Best
TEA SHOP WALKS
in
OXFORDSHIRE

Julie Meech

Published by Sigma Leisure – an imprint of
Sigma Press, 1 South Oak Lane, Wilmslow, Cheshire SK9 6AR, England.

British Library Cataloguing in Publication Data
A CIP record for this book is available from the British Library.

ISBN: 1-85058-636-5

Typesetting and Design by: Sigma Press, Wilmslow, Cheshire.

Cover photograph: Benson Lock *(Julie Meech)*

Maps and photographs: Julie Meech

Printed by: MFP Design and Print

Acknowledgement

Grateful thanks are due to Martin Browne of Stagecoach Oxford for generous help with travel costs.

Contents

The Walks

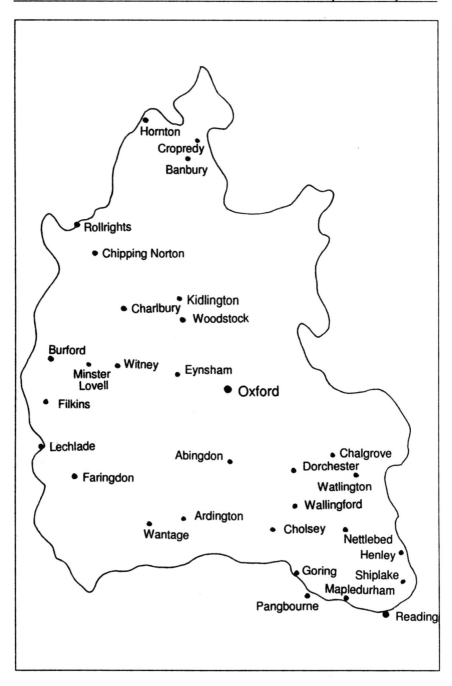

Oxfordshire

Oxfordshire's varied countryside is threaded by a network of over 2 300 miles (3 680km) of public rights of way, most of them signposted, waymarked and well-maintained. Plenty of scope for the walker then – and many local residents are well aware of that. Yet Oxfordshire is not so often thought of by visitors as a good destination for country walking, and is not so well known in this respect as it should be.

This may be partly because the county is overshadowed by Oxford itself. By any standards, Oxford is a remarkable city, known all over the world for its architectural treasures and its historical, educational and literary associations. The overwhelming abundance of attractions in the city does tend to eclipse the less obvious delights of what is, after all, unspectacular countryside.

Perhaps, too, many people are unaware of just how much Oxfordshire does encompass. Maybe they think in terms of the pre-1974 county, not realising that the Local Government Act of that year plundered huge swathes of Berkshire and bestowed them on its neighbour. Whatever Berkshire folk thought about that, and whatever any of us think about bureaucratic meddling and the creation of artificial boundaries, it's undeniable that Berkshire's loss was immeasurably Oxfordshire's gain. Much of what is now best about Oxfordshire was actually taken from Berkshire, including a large chunk of what we still refer to as the Berkshire Downs.

Perhaps it is also true that there is a certain lack of cohesion about Oxfordshire, which causes some confusion as to where it actually is. It's hard to put a label on a county which is shared between the midlands (Banbury), the south-west (the Cotswolds and the Wiltshire border country) and the home counties (the Chilterns). Yet this should only serve to underline that Oxfordshire is a county of impressive variety. In the north and west its share of the Cotswolds is substantial. While it does not compare in quantity or quality with Gloucestershire's share, it does include some thoroughly delightful but relatively undiscovered countryside in an area bounded by Chipping Norton, Woodstock, Witney and Burford, which are themselves as charming as one expects Cotswold towns to be. North of

Chipping Norton, there is more attractive countryside running up towards Edge Hill as the land falls from the limestone wolds to the plain around Banbury.

Banbury stands on the River Cherwell, which meanders dreamily, yet, in a way, purposefully, almost due south to join the Thames at Oxford. The construction of the M40 has destroyed the tranquillity of part of the Cherwell Valley, and the growth of Banbury itself continues unabated. All the same, there are some stretches of the Cherwell, especially where it runs in close company with the Oxford Canal, that are the equal of any lowland landscape in central England. And the villages are magnificent, packed with exquisite cottages built of the vibrant orange local ironstone.

To the south-east of Oxford the land rises again, to the glorious beechwoods and flower-rich chalk grasslands of the Chiltern Hills. Despite their proximity to Reading and London the Chilterns somehow contrive to remain mostly unspoilt, their woods and villages among the loveliest in England, while some exhilarating walking is guaranteed by the presence of the Ridgeway National Trail.

Before it turns north to traverse the Chiltern escarpment, the Ridgeway has already travelled east from Wiltshire along the crest of the Berkshire Downs, providing some of the finest walking in southern England and incomparable views over the Vale of White Horse and the Thames Valley. It is the Thames, of course, which is the best-known asset of Oxfordshire's countryside. As it meanders across the county from west to east, it is never without interest, beauty or variety, from the remote, tranquil calm of Kelmscott to the lively, colourful scenes of Henley's Regatta. Despite its popularity with walkers, anglers, picnickers and boaters, the Thames remains relatively rich in wildlife, and you can expect to see a good many water birds, not just mallards and moorhens, but also more spectacular species such as herons, kingfishers and great crested grebes.

Oxfordshire is not, on the whole, as rich in wildlife as less intensively cultivated counties, but it does have some surprises: buzzards, for instance, are now increasingly common in the Cotswolds, as they move steadily eastwards from their western stronghold, and the red kite, quite recently reintroduced to the Chilterns, is thriving once again. The flower-rich grasslands of the Chilterns are ideal places to watch butterflies, which occur in great numbers in a good summer. As far as mammals are concerned, you will see mainly rabbits, squirrels and deer, with perhaps the occasional fox. But keep a special lookout for the endearing water vole – Ratty of *Wind in the Willows* fame. Kenneth Grahame's book was set by the Thames, but water voles are increasingly rare today. You will be lucky to see one, though a quiet, patient wait on a relatively undisturbed stretch of riverbank may bring its reward. One mammal you are almost certain not to see is the elusive otter, but it's good to know that this once persecuted mammal is making a tentative comeback to the upper Thames.

Tea and Tea Shops

The world is estimated to drink one billion cups of tea daily; only water is more widely consumed. The Chinese have been drinking tea for 5000 years, believing it to diminish fatigue and improve mental and physical performance. Buddhist monks, who drink tea to help them stay awake during meditation, have long believed that it has curative powers. So perhaps it's not surprising that when the first shipment of tea reached Britain in 1658 it was regarded as a medicine. Drinkers were assured that it was "approved by all Physicians" and claims for its medical efficacy grew steadily. It became fashionable, and Queen Anne gave it a considerable boost when it became known she had replaced her breakfast ale with tea. For many years only the rich could afford it, but eventually it became available to all sectors of society. Gradually, its supposed medicinal properties were largely forgotten, though it was always seen as refreshing and restorative, and was routinely offered in cases of shock or distress. Then came the backlash: tea was bad for you; high in caffeine, it caused dehydration and hindered the absorption of minerals and vitamins. Coupled with this was the growing popularity of coffee. Tea became less fashionable, but for millions of people it remained a daily staple.

Today, the pendulum is swinging back. Coffee is trendier, but tea is the new wonder drink. It seems the Chinese were right all along: tea is, apparently, brimful of antioxidants, all keen to do battle with those free radicals which course through our bodies causing ageing and degenerative diseases. Tea may also help to lower cholesterol (though probably not if you drink it with full-fat milk) and is a natural source of flouride, potassium, manganese, selenium and zinc. Tea, it is claimed now, can even help protect against cancer and heart disease. Nothing is proven, and arguments rage about the ben-

efits of green tea versus black, tea with milk or with lemon, herb tea
and various speciality teas. Whatever the truth, tea shops abound
(and, of course, they all serve coffee too) and most small market
towns have at least one, as do quite a few villages. There's nothing to
beat going for a walk in the country, but if you can combine it with a
drink and a snack in a tea shop, so much the better. All the tea shops
in this book fulfil certain criteria and all have been visited by the author (well, someone's got to do it). They span a wide spectrum, but
one thing they all have in common is a willingness on the part of the
owners to be included in this book. You can be certain, therefore
(barring a change of ownership), that walkers are welcome at all of
these tea shops. But please be considerate if wearing muddy boots
and dripping waterproofs. Children are welcome at all of them too,
but some owners did specify that they must be well-behaved. Dogs
are not generally welcome, but there are exceptions. Just see each individual entry for full details. Opening hours are given for each tea
shop, but these can vary so you may wish to check in advance (telephone numbers are given). Almost all cater for vegetarians to some
extent, however limited, but it's always a good idea to ask for details.
Apart from ensuring you're not unwittingly consuming lard or
chicken stock, it also helps to make proprietors aware of the growing
demand for vegetarian food. Finally, a word of warning: tea shops
change hands, relocate or close down, just like other business ventures, and a book takes many months to go from the research stage to
the bookseller's shelf. So it is possible that by the time you read this
not every establishment detailed will still be trading. If it's important to you, ring up to check. In most cases, however, there are pubs
and shops offering alternative sources of refreshment, and, quite often, other tea shops too.

The Walks

None of the walks in this book is particularly demanding for most
averagely fit people, and most are very gentle indeed. It's still as well
to be properly equipped, which means always taking waterproofs
with you, and sufficient layers of warm clothing in winter. It's best
not to wear jeans if rain threatens as they're uncomfortable when
wet and take ages to dry. Proper walking boots are not essential for
any of these walks, but they do provide good ankle support, and they
keep your feet dry in wet or muddy conditions. That is probably the

main reason for wearing them in Oxfordshire, where there is no rugged terrain, but where mud is always a consideration. All of the walks in this book are potentially very muddy, except after long spells of dry weather. In many cases you will encounter flooding when undertaking walks in the valleys of the Thames, Windrush and Evenlode during the winter.

Ordnance Survey maps are invaluable. The directions in this book should ensure you don't get lost, but maps enable you to make changes to the given route, to identify distant hills and to put the local scene in a wider context. Landranger maps are ideal for an overview, but the more detailed Pathfinder, Explorer and Outdoor Leisure maps are superb companions on any walk. The Pathfinder series is currently being replaced by Explorer maps, each of which covers a larger area and represents tremendous value for money. Most of the Oxfordshire ones are already available and the remaining few will be in the shops very soon.

All the walks in this book have been carefully checked, but things do change. Trees can be blown over, hedges ripped out, stiles moved, cottages bulldozed and bungalows erected. Any of these might make the directions invalid at some point but you're unlikely to encounter any real difficulties, especially as most of Oxfordshire's paths are in good order. Most are waymarked, with yellow arrows for footpaths, blue arrows for bridleways.

Oxfordshire County Council publishes a useful leaflet outlining rights and responsibilities pertaining to rights of way and this may be obtained from the Countryside Service, Department of Leisure and Arts, Holton, Oxford OX33 1QQ. (Tel. 01865 810226). Queries about footpaths (for instance, if you find one obstructed) should be addressed to the Rights of Way Office, Department of Leisure and Arts, Central Library, Westgate, Oxford OX1 1DJ. (Tel. 01865 810808).

Long-distance paths

Long-distance paths and other specially designated and waymarked routes have proliferated in recent years. All the routes listed below are encountered, however briefly, in the walks described in this book.

D'Arcy Dalton Way: 65 miles/105km; from Wormleighton Reservoir in Warwickshire to Wayland's Smithy on the Ridgeway.

Oxford Canal Walk: 83 miles/133km; pursues a rural route between Oxford and Coventry along the towpath of the Oxford Canal.

Oxfordshire Way: 68 miles/110km; from Bourton-on-the-Water in Gloucestershire to Henley-on-Thames, connecting the Heart of England Way with the Thames Path, and the Cotswolds with the Chilterns.

Ridgeway National Trail: 85 miles/137km; from Overton Hill near Avebury, along the North Wessex Downs and the Chilterns to Ivinghoe Beacon near Tring. It connects with the Icknield Way and the Wessex Ridgeway and is based on a prehistoric highway often known as "the oldest road".

Thames Path National Trail: 180 miles/288km; follows the River Thames from its source at Thames Head in Gloucestershire to the Thames Barrier at Woolwich in London's Docklands.

Countryside Stewardship

In the course of some of these walks you will encounter areas of land which are part of the Countryside Stewardship scheme. Administered by the Ministry of Agriculture, the scheme offers payments to farmers and landowners to enhance and conserve landscapes, wildlife and ancient monuments. Agreements usually run for 10 years, and while public access is not a requirement, it is encouraged. All the stewardship sites you will discover while doing these walks have public access and you are free to explore them. At the entry point to each site there are notices and detailed maps showing permitted access areas and footpaths.

BBONT (Berks, Bucks and Oxon Nature Trust)

The Trust is the leading local environmental charity and one of 47 independent charities which form a national partnership – the Wildlife Trusts – with over a quarter of a million members and 2000 nature reserves throughout the UK. BBONT manages over 90 nature reserves for the benefit of wildlife and enjoyment by people. If you'd like to discover more about local wildlife, or participate in activities or guided walks BBONT can be contacted at The Lodge, 1 Armstrong Road, Littlemore, Oxford OX4 4XT. (Tel. 01865 775476).

Tourist Information Centres

Abingdon: 01235 522711

Banbury: 01295 259855

Burford: 01993 823558

Chipping Norton: 01608 644379

Faringdon: 01367 242191

Henley-on-Thames: 01491 578034

Oxford: 01865 726871

Wallingford: 01491 826972

Wantage: 01235 760176

Witney: 01993 775802

Woodstock: 01993 811038

Public transport

Surely all country walkers must have noticed that it's now almost impossible, in England and Wales, to escape the sound of traffic? Or to find a view unspoilt by cars. Or a village not choked by them. And who has not gone back to somewhere they once loved, only to find it has been obliterated by a swathe of tarmac bypassing some traffic-battered little country town? With the Countryside Commission predicting a doubling, or even trebling, of rural traffic, things can only get worse. People talk of spending time in the countryside to find "peace and quiet" and to "get away from it all" and yet they go there by car, thereby helping to destroy the very thing they're in search of, and providing ammunition for the arguments of those who would build yet more bypasses. It doesn't have to be that way. It's easy, cheap and fun to get around by public transport, and that's how all the walks in this book were accessed. Why not give it a try?

Getting to Oxfordshire: Oxford is the main hub for bus and train services to the rest of the county, and is very easy to get to, with trains, buses and National Express coaches providing abundant services from around the country. For Londoners, in particular, a day in the Oxfordshire countryside is very easily achieved, with fast trains running frequently. It's slower by coach, of course, but with both Stagecoach Oxford (Oxford Tube) and Oxford Bus Company (Citylink) operating 24 hours a day, 365 days a year, who could possibly complain? Services run every 12 minutes at peak times, and even in the middle of the night the frequency never drops below hourly. Advance booking is not required and through tickets can be bought to destinations beyond Oxford, changing to local buses at Gloucester Green bus station.

Getting around Oxfordshire: there are frequent, fast and reliable train services to places such as Banbury, Henley, Goring etc. Bus services are somewhat sparse in the north of the county but elsewhere they are extraordinarily good. Some local services – Oxford to Abingdon, for instance, operate 24 hours a day, and local frequency is just as impressive – Oxford to Witney every 10 minutes, for example.

Information and fares: the information about public transport given for each walk in this book is accurate at the time of writing, but is incomplete. Only the most useful services are included, and there are often other local buses. Nor should it be relied upon unquestioningly because services can change at short notice (usually for the better, these days) so check before travelling, if possible.

Oxfordshire County Council publishes a series of 12 public transport guides which contain timetables and a map. You can pick them up in libraries or tourist information centres, or write to Oxfordshire County Council, Environmental Services, Speedwell House, Speedwell Street, Oxford OX1 1NE, enclosing a large SAE and stating which area you are interested in.

Individual bus and train operators produce their own timetables and promotional literature so visits to Oxford's Gloucester Green bus station and the rail station are recommended. Many libraries, tourist information centres, travel shops and rail stations have reference copies of the Great Britain Bus Timetable, published by Southern Vectis Bus Company, Nelson Road, Newport, Isle of Wight PO30 1RD. (Tel. 01983 522456). Most also have National Express and train timetables.

Individual fares vary considerably. Some are surprisingly low, others seem high. But there is a huge range of discount tickets for unlimited travel which mean the more you travel the cheaper it gets. They are offered by several companies and can be valid for individuals or families and for varying periods from a day to a year. Stagecoach Oxford has the biggest choice. Some are valid on the services of more than one operator – the Sunday Rover, for instance, allows unlimited travel through nine counties, including Oxfordshire, by bus and train. Integrated bus-rail ticketing is now commonplace – that is, you can buy bus/rail tickets on both buses and trains. Your bus or rail ticket can also gain you discounts on entry to various attractions.

Useful telephone numbers for public transport information:

Chiltern Queens: 01491 680354

National Express: 0990 808080

National Rail Enquiries: 0345 484950 (24 hours)

Oxford Bus Company: 01865 785400

Oxfordshire County Council: 01865 810405

Reading Buses: 0118 959 4000

Stagecoach Midland Red: 01788 535555

Stagecoach Oxford: 01865 772250 (24 hours)

Stagecoach Swindon & District: 01793 522243

Swanbrook Coaches: 01452 712386

Thames Travel: 01491 874216

Thamesdown Transport: 01793 42842

Worth's Motor Services: 01608 677322

Wycombe Bus Company: 01494 520941

Walk 1: Oxford

Start/finish: Oxford Station; grid reference 505063.

Summary: This effortless circular walk is without gradients and suitable for almost everybody. It reveals a side of Oxford which very few visitors see, though residents are well acquainted with it. Despite the closeness of the route to the city, you're likely to see masses of wild birds and a variety of wild flowers. Please note that dogs must be kept under control in Port Meadow.

Length: 5½ miles/8km.

Maps: OS Landranger 164, OS Explorer 180.

Buses/coaches: Local and national operators provide very frequent services to Oxford; please see the public transport section of the introduction for details.

Trains: Frequent services operate daily from all over the country.

Parking: Choose one of the park and ride car parks on the edge of the city.

The Tea Shop

The Saddlebag (and the Nosebag Restaurant), 6-8 St Michael's Street, Oxford.

St Michael's Street is a quiet thoroughfare opposite the church of St Michael at the Northgate, whose Saxon tower (c1040) is Oxford's oldest building. It's close to the busy crossroads of Magdalen Street, Cornmarket Street, Broad Street and George Street. The Nosebag Restaurant is upstairs, while the ground floor houses The Saddlebag, ideal for a quick snack and a drink. Deservedly popular, it offers an excellent range of snacks, including omelettes, quiches, sandwiches and home-made soups. Breakfasts are available until late afternoon. Many items are suitable for vegetarians, including some delicious savoury snacks, mostly served with salad. Sandwich fillings come in a variety of unusual combinations and can be made to order. A tempting range of cakes, teabreads, scones, desserts and Italian ice creams is on offer and the choice of drinks is good too, including some unusual ones, such as elderflower cordial. Everything, except bread, is freshly made on the premises daily. Neither dogs nor smokers are permitted, and children are welcome only if well-behaved.

Open: 9.30am-5.30pm daily (The Nosebag Restaurant upstairs remains open until late evening, except on Mondays). Telephone: 01865 721033.

Oxford

The first students were starting to gather in Oxford during the early 12th century and by 1200 it was firmly established as England's first university town. Today the university comprises a federation of 41 independent colleges and halls, mostly occupying the sort of buildings which lend substance to Oxford's claim to be "one of the great architectural centres of the world". Most are usually open to the public and a shortlist of the best might include Christ Church, Merton, University and Magdalen. Other centres of academia include the Ashmolean Museum and the Bodleian Library, but Oxford is as much town as gown, and there's more to see than just centres of learning. Enough to keep you busy for weeks, in fact, and the best

Oxford from the top of Carfax Tower

starting point for getting to grips with it all is the tourist information centre near the bus station at Gloucester Green.

While Oxford is undoubtedly a magnificent city to explore on foot, this is not an urban walk, but an exploration of Oxford's rural face, providing an interesting and very pleasant contrast to the city's more famous sights.

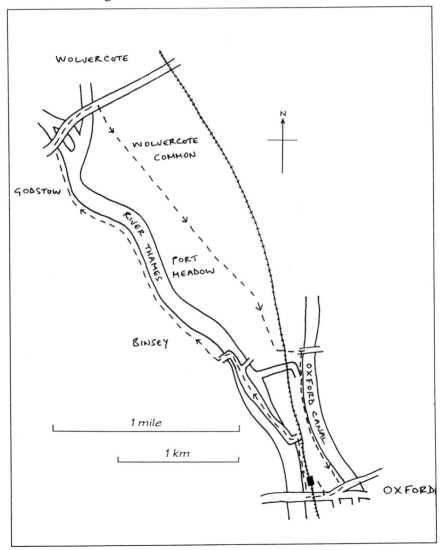

The Walk

Leave the station and turn right along Botley Road, then soon right again by the River Thames, joining the Thames Path. Before long you'll cross a footbridge and after this another channel keeps you company on your right, so that you're walking on a lushly vegetated strip of land between two water courses. Already, Oxford seems to have disappeared, as you enjoy glimpses of farmland on your left, and allotments on your right. The narrow strip of land broadens out to form Fiddler's Island, and there is a small marina here.

Pass a footbridge and continue to a second one, which takes you across the Thames to the west bank. Continue northwards, still on the Thames Path, passing Bossom's Boatyard. Across the river hundreds of horses, cattle and Canada geese graze on the large expanse of Port Meadow. On your left is the small settlement of Binsey, beyond it Wytham Hill and Wytham Great Wood. Only the roar of the concealed A34 spoils this pleasant place. Soon there is more open common on your left, grazed by cattle.

After Godstow Lock, you pass the remains of Godstow Nunnery, of which only the outer walls and the ruins of a chapel remain. Established in 1133, it became both prosperous and notorious; the nuns willingly entertained the young monks and students of Oxford and Henry II used to meet his mistress Rosamund Clifford here.

Go up to a road and leave the Thames Path, turning right over Godstow Bridge and past the Trout Inn (Inspector Morse's favourite). After crossing a second bridge you'll come to a car park/picnic site at Lower Wolvercote on the edge of Port Meadow and Wolvercote Common.

Port Meadow was used by our prehistoric ancestors and the slight eminence of Round Hill, which you will pass as you return towards Oxford, is the remains of a Bronze Age burial mound. In dry summers, crop marks show where huts and enclosures once stood. The meadow is thought to have been grazed for 4000 years without any ploughing or application of chemicals, and a profusion of wild flowers testifies to this. It's a good place to see birds too, especially in winter when flooding attracts flocks of waders, geese and ducks. Cattle and horses roaming the commons belong to the Freemen of Oxford and the Wolvercote Commoners who enjoy ancient grazing rights.

Make your way back towards Oxford, gradually bearing away

from the river towards the far side of Port Meadow, marked by a line of trees. As you draw level with Binsey you should be near the edge of the meadow, where you join a raised concrete path. Ignore a branching path and continue south until you can leave Port Meadow and turn left along a lane, crossing the railway then turning right to join the towpath of the Oxford Canal. Cross a black and white cast iron bridge and walk alongside the canal's terminal basin, with its colourful permanent moorings and waterside gardens. When you reach the road turn right for the station or left into Oxford.

Walk 2: Abingdon to Oxford

Start: The Square, Abingdon; grid reference 498971.

Finish: Folly Bridge, St Aldates, Oxford; grid reference 514055.

Summary: An easy linear walk on the Thames Path between Abingdon and Oxford. This may sound like an urban scenario, but Abingdon is left behind almost immediately and Oxford's suburbs make little impression, thanks to the green corridor pushed through the city by the River Thames.

Length: 8 miles/12.8km.

Maps: OS Landranger 164, OS Explorers 170 and 180.

Buses/coaches: Stagecoach Oxford buses operate a 24-hour service between Oxford and Abingdon, running frequently during the day. Cityline Buses also serve Abingdon and if you're arriving in Oxford by Thames Trains the "Oxford bus add-on" costs very little extra (ask for it when you buy your train ticket) and gives unlimited travel on Cityline Buses, including the X3 Abingdon Express. Buses also run to Abingdon from Didcot, Henley, Newbury, Wallingford and Wantage. For details about services to Oxford see the public transport section of the introduction.

Trains: Frequent services operate daily to Oxford. The nearest station to Abingdon is Radley.

Parking: Public car parks in Oxford or Abingdon.

The Tea Shop

Poppies, 37 Stert Street, Abingdon.

Popular with local people, Poppies is a friendly, cosy place with poppy-patterned curtains and a display of oil paintings decorating the walls. There's a comprehensive range of meals and snacks on offer and everything is home-made. Choose from all-day breakfasts, soups, curries, casseroles, omelettes, salads, ploughman's, pasta dishes, quiches, chillis, and much more. There are vegetarian options and a good range of cakes and ice creams, along with the usual hot and cold drinks. Smokers are welcome in a separate room. There is a garden at the back, but dogs are not permitted.

Open: 9.30am-4.00pm daily. Telephone: 01235 526600.

Abingdon

The largest town in the Vale of White Horse, Abingdon is built on the site of an Iron Age settlement and is generally acknowledged to be the oldest continuously inhabited town in England. It began as a trading centre and, much later, in the Saxon period, it developed rapidly after the building of an abbey in 675. The town's narrow streets still converge on the abbey site but only a few, mainly 15th-century, buildings survive of what was once a vast complex. Until 1974 Abingdon was in Berkshire and from 1556 to 1869 it was the county town. The former county hall, a majestic 17th-century building in The Square, now houses a museum. There are many other fine buildings in the town, and the 15th- and 18th-century almshouses near St Helen's Church are particularly beautiful. Nearby is The Wharf, where Jerome K Jerome's *Three Men in a Boat* tied up to visit The Anchor. Abingdon's riverside location helped it to become one of the chief centres of the Berkshire cloth trade, and the wharves were also busy with barges collecting locally produced malt bound for London, and delivering Somerset coal brought in on the now disused Wiltshire and Berkshire Canal.

Abingdon

The Walk

Leave The Square by walking between St Nicholas's Church and the Guildhall to join Abbey Close. Turn right, then right again on Checker Walk if you want to see the abbey buildings, but otherwise straight on. After passing a car park turn right to cross a millstream then left alongside the stream until a footbridge allows you to cross. Turn right on the Thames Path, through a lush landscape of meadowsweet, purple loosestrife, figwort, reeds and great willowherb, with the Thames at first hidden from view by the exuberance of the vegetation. Soon, however, it appears on your right, just before you pass an area of newly planted trees, dedicated as a community woodland, with picnic areas and permitted access for a 10-year period, ending in 2005.

The path stays close to the Thames, soon passing under the railway. There are flooded gravel pits to your left, while the trees of Lock Wood come down to the water's edge on the far bank. To the north of the wood is Nuneham Park, where Queen Victoria and Prince Albert spent their honeymoon. The impressive house, now a conference centre, was built in 1756 for Earl Harcourt of Stanton Harcourt.

Eventually, you arrive at Sandford-on-Thames, where two islands linked by a footbridge divide the river into two channels. Cross a footbridge onto the first island and walk past Sandford Lock. The village, beyond the lock, was once a small industrial centre. A corn mill was built by the Knights Templar in the 13th century, and its successor was later used for paper-making and all manner of other industrial processes, turning out fulled cloth, banknotes, metal pans, thimbles and flour. Sandford Mill closed in the 1970s.

The two river channels rejoin and a footbridge returns you to the left bank at Rose Isle, shortly after which the path splits but the two branches soon merge again by the river.

After going under a rail bridge the river again divides. The footpath follows the right channel, and a footbridge soon takes you across Iffley Lock then past the Isis Tavern. The Isis is an alternative name for the Thames (from the Latin Thamesis) which is used mainly in Oxford.

After the Isis Boathouse you'll see, on your left, a BBONT reserve, Iffley Meadows, ancient wet meadowland famous for its profusion of the nationally scarce snake's-head fritillary. There are also other plants of old meadowland, such as adder's-tongue fern, great burnet,

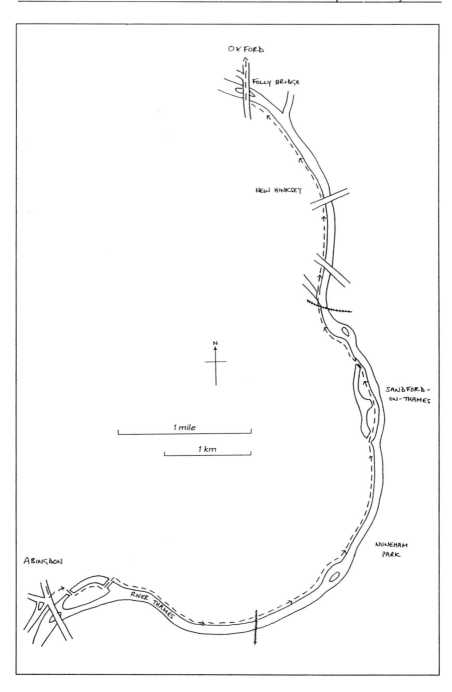

common meadow rue, pepper saxifrage, creeping jenny, marsh marigold, meadowsweet, ragged robin and oxeye daisy.

There are plenty of birds to be seen along this stretch, including greylag geese, Canada geese, mallards, moorhens, coots, herons, black-headed gulls and mute swans. Look out for long-horned cattle too, grazing in Christ Church Meadow on the far bank as you approach the city centre at The Head of the River (a pub) and Folly Bridge. If you leave the Thames here you'll find yourself on St Aldates, which provides a good route into the city centre, and is also well provided with bus stops for onward travel. Alternatively, you can stay by the river, following the Thames Path to Botley Road and the railway station.

Walk 3: Abingdon and Culham

Start/finish: The Square, Abingdon; grid reference 498971.

Summary: An easy circular walk which includes two delightful stretches of the
                     Thames Path and a visit to the attractive village of Culham. An optional
                     detour takes you into Sutton Courtenay, a larger village full of interest.

Length: 6½ miles/10.4km (plus 1½ miles/2.4km if exploring Sutton Courtenay).

Maps: OS Landranger 164, OS Explorer 170.

Buses/coaches: See Walk 2.

Trains: Nearest stations are Radley and Culham.

Parking: Public car parks in Abingdon.

The Tea Shop

The Gallery Tea Room, 25 Bridge Street, Abingdon.

This is a warm, friendly, unpretentious place offering excellent value for money and popular with local people. It's ideally situated next to the tourist information centre and close to the Thames. The wide range of meals includes all-day breakfasts, jacket potatoes, omelettes, daily specials, snacks on toast, sandwiches, cakes, ice creams, biscuits, tea cakes and much more. A dessert menu features a choice of wicked chocolatey feasts and there is also a special children's menu. The choice of drinks is equally good but no particular effort is made to cater for vegetarians, though a number of items available may be suitable – just ask for details if uncertain. The premises are non-smoking and no dogs, other than guide dogs, are permitted. The proprietors say that if a walking party wishes to meet at the tea room for breakfast they will open early if given 24 hours notice.

Open: 8.30am-5.00pm Tuesday, Wednesday, Thursday, Saturday; 9.00am-5.00pm Monday and Friday; 1.00pm-5.00pm Sunday. Telephone: 01235 538539.

Abingdon

For information about Abingdon please see Walk 2.

The Walk

Go down Bridge Street to cross the River Thames and when you reach a pink cottage turn left down steps to the river bank. Follow the Thames Path to Abingdon Lock, but leave it here (it crosses the lock), keeping straight on past the lock keeper's house, the river still on your left. When you come to a tributary stream follow it to a bridge. Having crossed, the path swings left between masses of thistles and willowherb – a major attraction for goldfinches in the autumn.

You soon come to the remains of Swift Ditch Lock, a milestone in the navigational history of the river, which had many shallows in this region, making it impassable to large craft. London-bound cargoes had to be hauled by wagon and packhorse along poor roads to Burcot before being loaded onto barges for the journey downstream. To improve navigation pound locks were built at Iffley, Sandford and Swift Ditch, replacing the earlier flash locks which were difficult and dangerous. For more than 150 years Swift Ditch was the main navigation channel of the Thames, but in 1790 the main navigation reverted to today's course through Abingdon, and Swift Ditch was left to earn its alternative name of Back Water.

Cross Swift Ditch and turn left to rejoin the Thames. When your way is eventually blocked by the railway turn right alongside it, climbing onto the slight rise of Culham Hill. One section of the path is overgrown with bracken and undermined by rabbits so take care not to twist an ankle. Joining a track at a railway bridge, turn right, passing a free-range pig farm. After passing the turn for Warren Farm House the track acquires a hard surface, becoming Thame Lane. It takes you past the former Culham College, now the European School, which was designed by the architect Joseph Clarke.

Reaching the main road, turn right, cross at traffic lights and go down Tollgate Road. When you come to the river again (not the main channel, but the Culham Cut, a man-made channel dug in 1809) turn right on the Thames Path by Culham Lock.

When you reach a footbridge over the river a footpath on the right leads into Culham. It's only a short distance and well worth the brief diversion. The old part of Culham comprises a handful of pleasant cottages by a green, Culham House, a pub, the 17th-century Manor House (with some extraordinary topiary in its garden) and St Paul's Church, which originated c1200 but was partially rebuilt in the 19th century by Joseph Clarke. Culham is an example of a shrunken village, the church and its neighbours being all that remain of a larger medieval settlement, revealed only by the outlines of streets, house platforms and trackways between the green and the river. Nobody knows why Culham was abandoned - possibly the Black Death or a series of poor harvests. A modern village has now grown up just to the east.

Return the same way to the Culham Cut and decide whether you want to make the detour to Sutton Courtenay. If so, cross the foot-

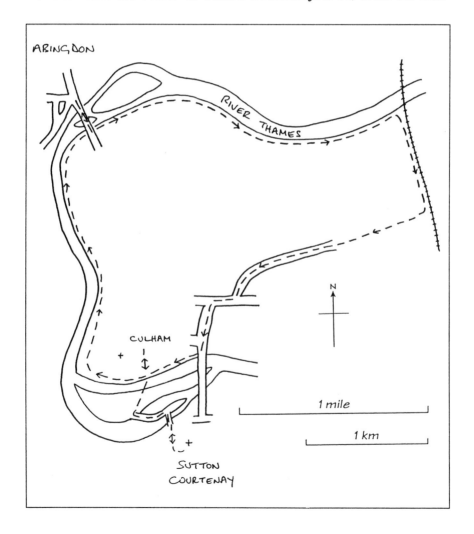

bridge and follow a well-trodden path through fields, over the main channel of the Thames and across Sutton Pools, crossing five bridges before you reach the village. There was a Royal palace here in the 11th century and even today a Norman house still survives on the main street, which is lined with a variety of beautiful period buildings in many different styles and materials. There are three pubs, a village green and All Saints' Church, an interesting building in its own right but best known for the fact that buried in the church-yard are Eric Arthur Blair (the real name of the writer George Orwell) and Herbert Henry Asquith, Earl of Oxford, and Liberal Prime Minister 1908-1916. It was in Sutton Courtenay that Asquith signed the papers declaring war on Germany in 1914 and it was to Sutton Courtenay that he retired in 1916.

Returning to the Thames Path, resume your walk towards Abingdon. As you approach the town you'll see a splendid cast iron bridge erected by the Wilts and Dorset Canal Company in 1824. Beyond this is St Helen's Wharf, where the church and three groups of almshouses are waiting to be explored.

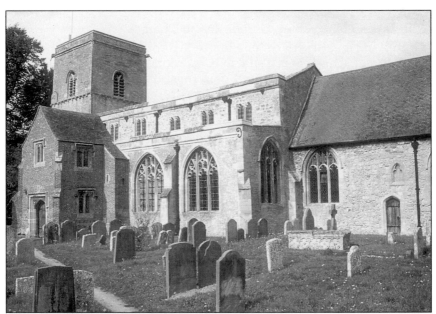

All Saints' Church, Sutton Courtenay

Walk 4: Dorchester

Start/finish: High Street, Dorchester; grid reference 578942.

Summary: A delightful circular walk from the former Roman town of Dorchester to the diminutive but distinctive Sinodun Hills, also known as Wittenham Clumps. It's very easy except for one short, steep climb and Dorchester is a beautiful village with a fine abbey church.

Length: 4½ miles/7.2km.

Maps: OS Landranger 164, OS Explorer 170.

Buses/coaches: Stagecoach Oxford 39 Abingdon to Wallingford via Dorchester, Monday to Saturday; X39 Oxford to Heathrow via Dorchester, daily; 105 Oxford to Wallingford via Dorchester, Monday to Saturday.

Trains: Nearest stations are Culham, Appleford and Didcot.

Parking: Public car park at south end of Dorchester (Bridge End).

The Tea Shop

Chesters, Queen Street, Dorchester on Thames.

Occupying an attractive stone house just round the corner from the High Street, Chesters is a spacious tea room, its beamed walls hung with a selection of prints and paintings. It offers a good choice of home-made cakes, scones, tea cakes, crumpets, toast, sandwiches and cream teas, along with a range of light lunches, from soups and pasties to pasta dishes and salads. All-day breakfasts are served and there is a daily special. A reasonably priced senior citizens' lunch is available from Monday to Friday. Vegetarians will find something suitable but should ask for details. The usual range of hot and cold drinks is available. Dogs are welcome, but not smokers, and walkers are asked to remove muddy boots.

Open: 9.30am-5.30pm daily in summer, 10.00am-5.00pm daily in winter. Telephone: 01865 341467.

Dorchester

This delightful place occupies a strategic position on the River Thame close to its junction with the River Thames and overlooked by the Sinodun Hills. Its well-drained, easily cultivated gravel soils made it a natural site for occupation by prehistoric man. Archaeological evidence reveals continuous settlement from c2500BC. It became an important Roman town and in the Saxon period was part of the kingdom of Wessex and probably the site of a Royal palace. In 635 Bishop Birinus, sent to England by the Pope, converted Cynegils, King of Wessex, to Christianity and founded a cathedral at Dorchester, which eventually became, in 869, the centre of a vast Mercian diocese stretching from the Thames to the Humber. By c1000 Oxford had taken over from Dorchester as the chief town of the upper Thames and after the Conquest the Normans moved the bishopric to Lincoln. In c1140 an abbey of Augustinian canons was founded by the Bishop of Lincoln on the site of Dorchester's former cathedral and the abbey church survives today.

The High Street is bordered by a variety of beautiful period buildings in stone, cob, flint, brick, timber, tile and thatch. Many of them were built, or rebuilt, in the 18th and 19th centuries when Dorchester was an important coaching stop on the London-Oxford road. To either side of the High Street is a network of lanes and paths worthy of exploration.

High Street, Dorchester

The Walk

Walk up the High Street towards Oxford then turn left on Watling Lane. As you pass allotments (occupying part of the site of the Roman town) join a footpath on the right, signposted to Day's Lock. It heads straight towards ramparts ahead, known as Dyke Hills, with the twin hills of Wittenham Clumps rising beyond. Dyke Hills were built to protect a late Iron Age settlement. The rivers Thame and Thames offered protection on three sides, and the earthworks of Dyke Hills completed the defences.

When you reach the ramparts turn right, and carry straight on at a cross track. The path soon bears left, crossing the ramparts, which are lower here. Passing through a gate, continue across a field with the River Thames on your right. Pass Day's Lock (the venue for the annual Poohsticks World Championships) and cross all three chan-

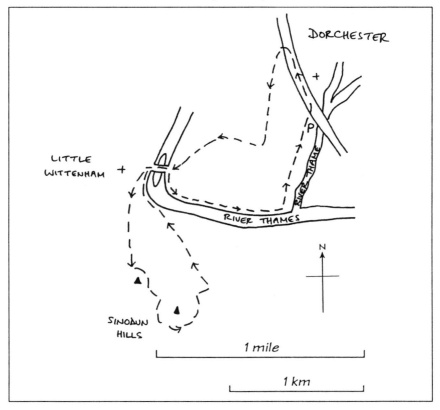

nels of the river then walk up a rough lane to Little Wittenham. Pass St Peter's Church (worth a visit first) and turn left into Church Meadow, entering a nature reserve run by the Northmoor Trust. A map here shows permitted footpaths which enable you to extend the walk if you wish.

The reserve is grazed by a small herd of Herefords, creating ideal conditions for specialist wildlife of chalk grassland and scrub. The idea is to use selective grazing to create a mosaic of different habitat types, with short, flower-rich grassland, rough grassland and scrub.

Take the footpath along the right-hand edge and climb steeply up Round Hill, turning left by the trees on top. Walk towards Castle Hill, to which a stile gives access, and climb to another clump of trees. This is the site of Sinodun Camp, an Iron Age fort which commands a fine view of the Thames Valley, the Chilterns, the Berkshire Downs and, of course, the inescapable Didcot Power Station.

Descend to the ramparts of the camp and follow them round anti-clockwise until a stile on your right gives access to a descending footpath along the outer edge of Little Wittenham Wood. Very soon, another stile lets you enter the wood and the path descends to a junction where you turn left, passing a pond then climbing up a gravelly track, soon bearing right off the track into the trees and bearing left at a junction with a bridleway. Turn left to return to Church Meadow and go diagonally across it to Little Wittenham and back across the Thames.

Join the Thames Path, turning right beside the river. When the tributary River Thame flows into its larger sibling, leave the Thames Path and turn left. Cross Dyke Hills and turn right along a footpath. Joining a track, Wittenham Lane, keep straight on towards Dorchester.

Walk 5: Wallingford

Start/finish: Market Place, Wallingford; grid reference 607894.

Summary: A thoroughly enjoyable circular walk which uses two short stretches of
                    the Ridgeway and visits the lovely village of North Stoke before taking
                    to the lower slopes of the Chilterns. There are no steep climbs.

Length: 7½ miles/12km.

Maps: OS Landranger 175, OS Explorer 171.

Buses/coaches: Stagecoach Oxford 39 Abingdon to Wallingford, Monday to Saturday;
                    X39 Oxford to Heathrow via Wallingford, daily; 105 Oxford to
                    Wallingford, Monday to Saturday; Reading Buses 105 Reading to
                    Wallingford, Monday to Saturday; Thames Travel 130 Didcot to
                    Wallingford, Monday to Saturday; 132 Watlington to Woodcote via
                    Wallingford, Monday to Saturday.

Trains: Nearest station is Cholsey.

Parking: Public car parks in Wallingford.

The Tea Shop

Annie's Tea Rooms, 79 High Street, Wallingford.

Annie's is at the east end of the High Street and its narrow street
frontage means it's easily missed. Inside, however, there's plenty of
space and it proves to be a traditional tea room where lunches are
served between 12.00 and 2.30 and the menu includes such staples
as jacket potatoes, salads, home-made soups and a hot dish of the
day. Everything is freshly prepared. Vegetarian choices are available
and the salads are excellent. Morning coffee and afternoon tea are
just as good, with scones, cakes, tea cakes and toast to choose from.
The usual selection of drinks is augmented by a good choice of speciality and herb teas. Not surprisingly, Annie's is a member of the
Tea Council Guild of Tea Shops. The premises is non-smoking, dogs
are welcome and parties should book in advance.

Open: 10.00am-5.00pm Monday, Tuesday, Thursday, Friday, Saturday; 2.30pm-5.30pm Sundays in July, August, September. Telephone: 01491 836308.

Wallingford

Enviably situated below the Chilterns and the Berkshire Downs, Wallingford is a delightful small town. It developed at the point where the Icknield Way forded the Thames and it later grew into the largest of Alfred the Great's fortified towns. Much of the Saxon street pattern still survives but most of the buildings are from the 17th and 18th centuries. In 1066 William the Conqueror forded the Thames at Wallingford, on his way from victory at Hastings to coronation at Westminster, via a roundabout route in which he allowed his men to pillage the countryside. He ordered the building of a substantial castle, completed in 1071, the ruins of which may still be seen. In 1154

the castle was the venue for the signing of the Treaty of Wallingford, which brought to an end the civil war between King Stephen and Empress Matilda. The following year Stephen's successor Henry II granted the town its royal charter, and Wallingford claims to be the oldest royal borough in the country. Viewers of the television detective series *Midsomer Murders* will recognise Wallingford, which has featured in the series as a backdrop to the not-very-impressive deductive powers of John Nettles' Inspector Barnaby.

The River Thames at Wallingford

The Walk

Begin in the Market Place and pass to the left of the 17th-century Town Hall then soon left on Hart Street. Turn right, left through a car park then right again along Riverside, which leads to St Leonard's Lane, where you turn left at the sign for the Thames Path.

Go through a boatyard and on along a paved path beside gardens, then past fields grazed by shaggy Highland cattle. As you approach a road bridge bear right to go up to it and turn left over the river. A path on the left leads to a subway which enables you to go under the road, joining the Ridgeway bridleway. Cross the Ridgeway footpath, and go straight on, heading south parallel with the Thames.

When you reach Carmel College at Mongewell Park a right turn allows you to visit St John's Church if you wish; otherwise keep straight on. You'll pass poplar plantations, a golf course, scrub, a nature reserve and wetland areas before you come to The Old Mill at North Stoke. Continue through this pretty village, with its harmonious mix of brick, tile, flint and thatch, to reach a junction. The Ridgeway turns right here on Church Lane (St Mary's Church, built c1230, is worth a visit) but our route is straight on along The Street until it becomes Pickets Lane, where you turn left past The Grange.

At a crossroads, go straight on towards Ipsden, joining Whitehouse Road and climbing very gently between arable fields with sweeping views to rolling hills. At the next crossroads, continue straight on.

The road descends slightly to cross Trunk Ditch and Brockendon Bottom, then rises very gently. When a bridleway crosses the road turn left on it. The route is obvious, along the side of Coblers Hill and through Drunken Bottom, but don't miss the point at which it crosses to the other side of the hedge. Joining a road at a junction go straight on along a lane opposite. When you come to the point where the Ridgeway footpath crosses the road turn left on it, walking on a tree-lined path on a raised bank, part of the dyke and ditch construction known as Grim's Ditch. Running parallel with the Ridgeway for over 15 miles/24km, this is a prehistoric earthwork apparently dug as a defensive boundary to discourage the people of the vale from raiding the sheep and cattle of those living on the downs.

At the main road cross and turn right for a few paces to where the path can be rejoined. At a junction a little further on ignore a right fork and keep straight on along the main path. Reaching the road, a left turn takes you to the subway you used earlier. On the other side just keep straight on, passing a church and the buildings of Newnham Farm. When the track bears right join a footpath on the left. Go forward on this a little way until another path is indicated on the left, leading to the river. Follow the Thames towards Wallingford and pass under the bridge then up steps to cross the bridge and access the town. At the crossroads, you will find Annie's straight ahead, and the Market Place to the left.

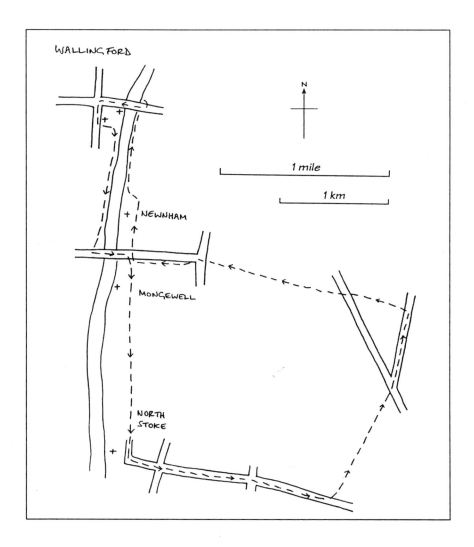

Walk 6: Wallingford to Dorchester

Start: Market Place, Wallingford; grid reference 607894.

Finish: Dorchester Abbey, Dorchester; grid reference 579943.

Summary: The Thames Path forms the bulk of the route on this easy linear walk which also includes the gorgeous village of Warborough, while both Dorchester and Wallingford are amply endowed with charm and character.

Length: 6½ miles/10.4km.

Maps: OS Landranger 164; OS Explorer 170.

Buses/coaches: Stagecoach Oxford 39 Abingdon to Dorchester and Wallingford, Monday to Saturday; X39 Oxford to Heathrow via Dorchester and Wallingford, daily; 105 Oxford to Dorchester and Wallingford, Monday to Saturday; Reading Buses 105 Reading to Wallingford, Monday to Saturday; Thames Travel 130 Didcot to Wallingford, Monday to Saturday; 132 Watlington to Woodcote via Wallingford, Monday to Saturday.

Trains: Nearest station is Cholsey.

Parking: Public car parks in Wallingford or Dorchester.

The Tea Shop

Dorchester Abbey Tea Room, Dorchester.

You'd go a long way to find a tea room with more character than this, which, appropriately enough, occupies the former guest house of the abbey. The historic building is stone at the front, timber-framed at the rear, with a cloister garden which is pleasant on sunny days. If using the beamed and panelled indoor room you must look for a spare seat at one of two large tables, decorated with fresh flowers and weighed down with plates of home-made cakes and scones. Tea is available by the cup from the ladies who staff the small kitchen and the more you drink the cheaper it gets. Prices are described as "variable"- at the time of writing (autumn 1998) your first cup of tea is 30p, your second is 25p, your 3rd is 20p and the 4th is up to you. The tea room is run on "liberal disciplinarian lines" and customers are invited to help themselves and then reckon up and pay for what they have eaten. Wasting food is "frowned upon" and "customers are exhorted not to take more butter and jam than they can eat. It is liable to render the proprietress violent". Children are welcome if accompanied by adults, and dogs are welcomed with enthusiasm. Smokers are "unwelcome and will be evicted immediately". No conscious attempt is made to cater for vegetarians but it's worth asking what's in the cakes as some may be suitable. All profits go to a variety of charities and over the last 20 years more than £100,000 has been donated.

Open: Wednesday, Thursday, Saturday and Sunday from 3.00pm until the food runs out; March to October. Telephone: 01865 340044.

Wallingford

For information about Wallingford please see Walk 5.

Benson Lock, River Thames

The Walk

From the Market Place head north into High Street and turn right towards the river. Just before you reach it turn left on the Thames Path at Castle Lane, and very soon turn right just past a pub. As you leave the town behind you pass the remains of the castle, which was completed in 1071.

When you reach Benson Lock cross the river and turn left. Quite soon, a footpath on the right allows you to cross through woodland and over a tributary stream. If you want to visit the village of Benson, which is full of lovely buildings, cross the busy main road with great care. Otherwise, stay on the Thames Path, which soon returns to the river near the Riverside Café and Shop. Walk past boats and caravans and on along the edge of cattle-grazed meadows, with pollarded willows gracing the far bank. At Shillingford Bridge turn right, go up to the road and cross to regain the footpath, which takes you to a lane. Turn right, passing some beautiful houses.

Leaving the Thames Path, cross the main road and go forward up Warborough Road, soon joining a footpath, which runs alongside the road to the right of a stream. After passing some charming cottages, you come to The Green South, where a short detour allows an exploration of one of the county's most delightful villages. There are gorgeous cottages, a pub ("the soon to be nearly famous Nelly's"), 13th-century St Luke's Church and the village green, where a sports pavilion bears the inscription "To the memory of the Rev Herbert White who saved this green from goths and utilitarians 1853".

The Green North takes you back to the road, where you turn right. When the road bends right go left at Sinodun View and immediately fork right on Hammer Lane. When the lane bends sharp right carry straight on along a bridleway, Priests' Moor Lane, to a T-junction with another track by the River Thame. Turn left, go under the bypass and stay on the track which meets a lane at the hamlet of Overy. Turn right on a footpath which takes you past 18th-century Overy Mill to Hurst Watermeadow, a nature reserve owned by a charitable trust. Interpretation boards on the site give details about this valuable wildlife habitat.

A footbridge at the far side gives access to a track. At a junction turn left and keep forward past Monks Close. At the next junction fork left on a narrow path before turning right to return to the lane,

then left on Queen Street and left again on High Street to Dorchester Abbey Tea Room.

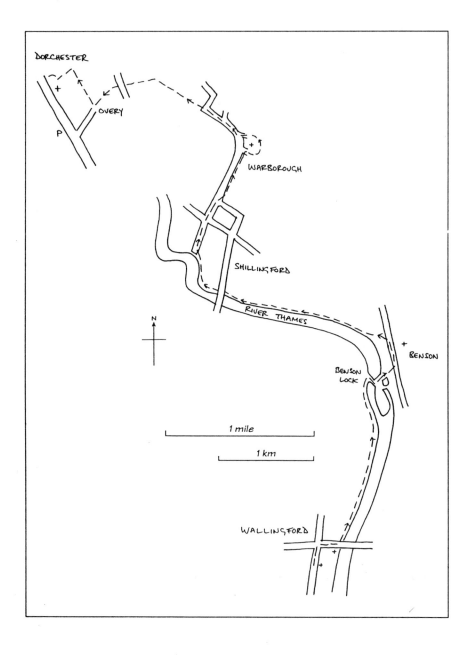

Dorchester Abbey

Dorchester was a significant site of early Christianity. It was here in 635 that King Cynegils of Wessex was converted by the Papal envoy Birinus. A church was built, and then a cathedral. This fell into disuse but in c1140 an abbey was founded on the same site. The abbey church was enlarged over the next two centuries, culminating in the building of the present chancel in 1340. This contains some magnificent windows, notably the Jesse window, which shows the family tree of Jesus. After the Dissolution in 1536 the abbey church was purchased for £140 by Richard Beauforest who gave it to the parish. The only monastic building to survive was the abbey guesthouse, now the tea room. There is much of human interest in the church – look for the memorial telling the sad story of an abandoned wife whose "nerves were too delicately spun to bear the rude shakes and jostlings which we meet with in this transitory world". Look too for the rare lead font, the sleeping monks corbel, Sir John de Holcombe's superb tomb, and much, much more. And for more information about Dorchester please turn to walk 4.

Walk 7: Goring

Start/finish: Goring & Streatley Station; grid reference 603806.

Summary: A beautiful circular walk on the edge of the Chilterns, using short lengths of two national trails, the Ridgeway and the Thames Path, as well as a variety of other well-defined rights of way. There are plenty of ups and downs but nothing too strenuous.

Length: 9 miles/14.5km.

Maps: OS Landranger 175, OS Explorer 171.

Buses/coaches: Reading Buses 105 Reading to Wallingford via Streatley, Monday to Saturday; Thames Travel 132 Watlington to Woodcote via Goring, Monday to Saturday; Thames Travel 137 Abingdon to Goring, Sundays only; Chiltern Queens operates a number of less frequent local services; Weavaway Travel X48 (Ridgeway Explorer) Reading to Wantage via Goring, Sundays/BHMs from April to October.

Trains: Thames Trains operates daily services between Oxford and Paddington via Goring & Streatley.

Parking: Pay and display car park at the station.

The Tea Shop

Riverside Tea Rooms, Bridge Approach, High Street, Goring.

Ideally situated by the Thames, with a garden and patio, Riverside Tea Rooms is a pleasant place for a break whether you sit outside or in the spacious, light and sunny interior, which is decorated with local paintings. The menu includes a wide range of snacks such as soups, pasties, jacket potatoes, pizza, breakfasts, sandwiches and toasted sandwiches, as well as the usual cakes, scones and cream teas. Soups, pasties and cakes are all home-made. There are a few vegetarian options and free-range eggs are used. A take-away service is available and ice creams are popular in summer. Smoking is not permitted but dogs are welcome in the garden.

Open: 10.00am-5.00pm Monday to Friday; 10.00am-6.00pm weekends. Easter to end of October. Telephone: 01491 872243.

Goring

The gap between the Chilterns and the Berkshire Downs through which the Thames flows at Goring was formed by meltwater from an ice sheet. For thousands of years huge volumes of water wore away the soft chalk to form the Goring Gap, marking the change from the wide, flat Oxford plain upstream to the steeper-sided valley downstream. The Goring Gap may be the oldest Thames crossing, used by two major prehistoric trade routes, the Ridgeway and the Icknield Way. Villages grew up on both sides of the crossing and in Anglo-Saxon times the river formed a frontier between Wessex (on the Streatley side) and Mercia. Streatley was the larger village and remained so until the railway was built through Goring, which subsequently expanded, while Streatley, hemmed in by steep slopes, did not.

The Walk

Leave the station from platform 4 and turn right past the car park to join Gatehampton Road. Very soon, you're in open country, with the tree-clad Chiltern foothills rising to your left, and the Berkshire Downs beyond the Thames on your right.

Turn right on a bridleway to Gatehampton Nurseries and keep more or less straight on at all junctions, soon joined by the Thames Path, which has taken a less direct route from Goring. The bridleway runs through woodland by the river then climbs steadily into higher, more open country.

When eventually the bridleway joins a road cross over and turn left, leaving the Thames Path and climbing steadily uphill on a footpath just above the road. When you reach Firhill cross to the war memorial and keep going uphill a little way to join a path which climbs above the road to a gate into a field. Turn left along its edge, eventually joining a green lane which runs towards Beech Farm.

After passing the main farm buildings bear left to a footpath and go forward along the edge of a paddock to enter Beech Wood. The path leads to a junction where you fork left. Go over a stile and straight on over an arable field to another stile at the far side. Walk to the far right corner of the next field and over a stile concealed in the hedge. Turn left across another field and then right along a farm track.

When you reach a lane cross to join a bridleway opposite, which takes you to another lane where you turn right. Join the next bridleway on the left, by Laurel Cottage. After passing Lavender Cottage the bridleway plunges into woodland, descending into the valley known as Blackbird's Bottom. Reaching a track, join a footpath opposite which climbs briefly then follows a well-trodden course to the road. Cross to another bridleway opposite, next to Little Heath. Descending between Park Wood and Old Elvendon Wood, you arrive at Elvendon Lane, where you turn left for a short distance before

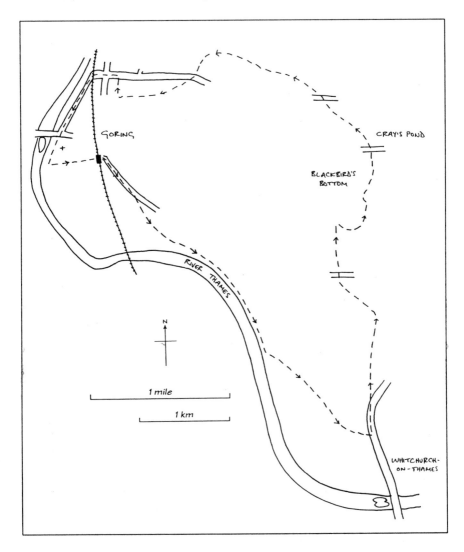

joining another bridleway on the right. At a junction just keep straight on along the bridleway, enjoying lovely views of the rolling downs above Goring and Streatley.

The bridleway enters Wroxhills Wood and eventually forks. Take the left-hand branch, soon descending along the edge of the wood and down to Battle Road (the continuation of Elvendon Lane). Cross to another path almost opposite and follow it to Goring. Coming out on a lane by a bungalow go forward across a strip of grass to a cycleway and turn right. This takes you back to Battle Road where you turn left, soon crossing the B4009 and passing under the railway to reach Cleeve Road. Turn left (now on the Ridgeway) and follow the road to Cleve Mead where you join a footpath on the right. This leads to Thames Road where you keep forward to reach Bridge Approach at the end of the High Street.

Turn right to find the Riverside Tea Rooms. To return to the station cross the road to rejoin the Thames Path which takes you past the attractive Goring Mill Gallery to the river. Turn left and, soon after crossing a footbridge, left again over a grassed area to join Ferry Lane, which leads to Station Road.

Goring Lock on the River Thames

Walk 8: Goring to Cholsey

Start:	Goring & Streatley Station; grid reference 603806.
Finish:	Cholsey Station; grid reference 584860.
Summary:	A delightful linear walk which ventures briefly out of Oxfordshire to sample a stretch of the Berkshire Downs, while also including fine views of the Chilterns, providing a clear illustration of the contrast between these two landscapes either side of the Goring Gap, where the walk begins.
Length:	7½ miles/12km.
Maps:	OS Landranger 175, OS Explorer 170.
Buses/coaches:	See Walk 7 for details of buses to Goring.
Trains:	Thames Trains operates daily services between Oxford and Paddington via Goring & Streatley and Cholsey.
Parking:	Pay and display car parks at the two rail stations.

The Tea Shop

Jan-Marie Bakery and Tea Room, 9 The Arcade, High Street, Goring.

Though this is primarily a village bakery, floor space has been given over to a simple tea room with five round tables, each decorated with fresh flowers. The friendly staff will serve you with anything from the patisserie counter or make up fresh sandwiches with your choice from a range of interesting fillings. Savouries and pastries are also available, as well as toasted tea cakes and cream teas. Drinks include a choice of different coffees and speciality teas, fruit juices and canned drinks. The tea comes in generous pots. Every effort will be made to provide for vegetarians – just ask the staff if you're unsure about the suitability of anything. There is no smoking and dogs are not permitted. However, they may be tied up outside using the hooks provided.

Open: 8.30am-5.00pm Monday to Saturday; 11.30am-5.00pm Sunday. Telephone: 01491 874264.

Goring

For information about Goring please see Walk 7.

Streatley

Streatley lies on the Icknield Way, a prehistoric trade route which ran from the south west to Norfolk but has largely, though not entirely, been absorbed into the modern road network. For much of its way it follows a line just to the north of the Ridgeway, though in places the two coincide. Streatley was formerly more important than neighbouring Goring but, when the railway was built through Goring, the latter expanded. Streatley remains small and undeveloped, though it's busy with traffic. The main street is lined with attractive houses, mainly of brick, but with some flint and half-timbering too.

The River Thames at Streatley

The Walk

Leave the station via platform 1 and go straight ahead down a lane, passing an old barn. Take the first right, just after a Community Centre, and walk to The Arcade, where the tea shop is situated. Turn left down the High Street and join the Ridgeway, crossing the River Thames into Streatley, and Berkshire. Keep straight on to a T-junction then turn right and shortly fork left beside the Wantage road (A417). Before long branch left on Rectory Road. A little way along here a path on the left gives access to the National Trust's Lough Down – well worth the short detour in early summer when the short chalky turf is rich in wild flowers. Just beyond it is Lardon Down, similarly flower-rich and also owned by the Trust.

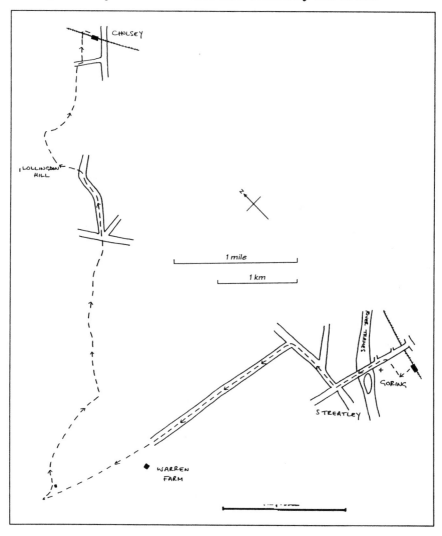

To continue with the walk, however, just keep following the Ridgeway which eventually bears right by the entrance to Warren Farm and begins its gentle climb onto the downs. Warren Farm is run by the Kulika Charitable Trust which provides "sustainable agriculture training for Africa" – one can't help but be struck by the irony of this when considering the way the Berkshire Downs have been transformed by chemicals and so-called "improvement" into the prairie-like monoculture which prevails today. Perhaps it is the British agri-barons who should be taking lessons in sustainability from African peasant farmers. However, at least Warren Farm is operating organically and produce is on sale from the farm shop.

When the path levels out and you arrive at a triangular junction leave the Ridgway and turn right on another footpath which soon enters the Well Barn Estate. Turn left over a stile just before you reach a house. As you do so you return to Oxfordshire and you also enter an attractive wood, predominantly beech but with a sprinkling of wild cherry, holly, silver birch and sycamore. Primroses and bluebells bloom profusely in the spring. There are two footpaths here; take the right-hand one and follow it through the trees to a clearing and a junction. Carry straight on along a stony track, with Unhill Wood on your left, Cow Common and Ham Wood to your right.

Eventually a signpost indicates a footpath and this is your cue to branch left. The path first crosses a grassy bank where thyme, trefoil and wild strawberries bloom in early summer. It then plunges into woodland, soon descending quite steeply before climbing up again, to deliver a fine view of the Chilterns, which, sadly, will soon be hidden by the newly planted trees on the right. After this point the path begins a long descent towards a farm in the valley below. At a junction turn right towards the farm then go over a stile on the left into sheep pasture. Go obliquely left, through a gap in a hedge and on in the same direction, the hedge on your left, to reach a stile to a track. Turn right, cross the main road with care and take the left-hand one of two lanes opposite. Just after the lane bends right join a bridleway on the left. It soon turns right to pass Lollingdon Hill and continues to a junction near Lollingdon Farm. Turn right here on a field-edge bridleway. At a junction by Westfield Farm keep straight on. Coming out on a track by Blooms Cottage turn right then left towards the railway ahead. After tunnelling under the line, turn right to Cholsey Station.

Walk 9: Mapledurham

Start/finish: Mapledurham; grid reference 671769.

Summary: This very short but quite lovely circular walk in the Chilterns takes you through beechwoods and over grassland. The village of Mapledurham is a thoroughly delightful little place by the north bank of the Thames between Whitchurch and Caversham.

Length: 4½ miles/7.2km.

Maps: OS Landranger 175, OS Explorer 171.

Buses/coaches: Chiltern Queens services from Woodcote and Reading to Goring Heath Post Office, Monday to Saturday.

Trains: Nearest stations are Pangbourne and Reading.

Parking: Mapledurham Country Park or find a space by the roadside – probably at Goring Heath rather than Mapledurham.

The Tea Shop

Mapledurham Tea Shop, Mapledurham House and Mill, Mapledurham.

There are only two tea rooms in this book where an entry charge is payable, and this is one of them. There is a charge to enter the grounds even if you don't have a car to park and don't wish to visit the two main attractions, namely Mapledurham House and the nearby watermill. At the time of writing (autumn 1998) the charge is £3.00 per person but is subject to review. The tea shop is housed in the 14th-century Old Manor, in a former stable block which now has a brightly painted interior and trestle tables, while more seating is available outside at picnic tables from which you may enjoy a pleasant view of the Thames. A range of cakes, scones and cream teas is available, together with the usual choice of drinks. No conscious attempt is made to cater for vegetarians but it may be worth asking for details as some of the cakes may be suitable. Dogs are welcome, but only at the outside tables, and there is no smoking.

Open: 12.30am-5.00pm weekends and bank holidays. Easter to end of September. Telephone: 0118 9723350.

Mapledurham House and Mill

Elizabethan Mapledurham House is a magnificent building, inside and out, and enjoys a number of literary connections: with Alexander Pope, Galsworthy's *Forsyte Saga* and Kenneth Grahame's *Wind in the Willows* (as the model for Toad Hall). It has also featured in a number of television dramas, including *Inspector Morse* and Joanna Lumley's *Class Act*. In 1971 sequences for *The Eagle has Landed*, starring Michael Caine, were filmed at Mapledurham. The mill was used for a dramatic scene in which one of the German soldiers is caught on the millwheel. In real life, Mapledurham Mill is the only working flour mill left on the Thames. The present building dates from the 15th century, though there has been a mill on this site since Saxon times.

The Walk

Walk up the north-bound lane (i.e. not towards either Caversham or Whitchurch) from Mapledurham until you come to a bridleway signed to Goring Heath. This leads to Bottom Farm and you should continue past the farm, forking left so that you stay on the bridleway. Pass to the right of a patch of woodland then keep forward until a bridle gate gives access to Bottom Wood, with beech, ash and maple, and a rich ground cover of wild flowers.

When the path forks (just after you've passed a footpath coming from the left) go to the right, past a grove of beeches. You'll soon come to an area of laurels and a distinctive beech with a bare trunk topped by a cluster of branches. The path forks again here and you should take the left-hand option, a holloway flanked initially by laurels then by mixed woodland.

Pass between two houses, Holly Copse and Holly Copse Cottage, to reach a track where you turn left. Ignore a bridleway and footpath indicated on the left and stay on the main track, which is lined with cherry and walnut trees.

Just after Cherry Tree Cottage fork left on an unmade road, which soon becomes a narrow bridleway. Ignore any branching paths and stay on this tree-lined route between fields. It brings you out at a road by the former Goring Heath Post Office (which is also a former tea room). Cross the road, going forward towards Checkendon and Petard. There's a bus stop here and this is where you start the walk if arriving by bus.

A little beyond the bus stop join a footpath on the right which follows a farm drive for a short distance until a stile gives access to sheep pasture. Turn left along its edge, passing an attractive flint and timber farmhouse. Cross a track to enter another field and walk towards a beechwood ahead.

Entering the wood, go forward and keep straight on at two junctions. At the far side of the wood intercept another path and turn right, following white arrows painted on the trees. Reaching the edge of the wood, it's right again for a few paces, and again when the path forks.

Keep straight on now, soon walking along the edge of the wood

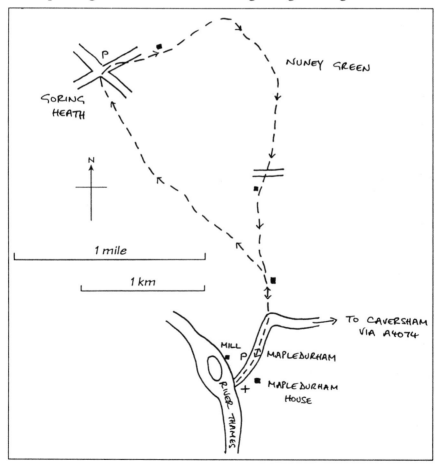

with a field on your left. Reaching a pond, go forward to pass to the left of it and then immediately turn right, still following the white arrows. The path leads away from the pond, soon passing a beautiful thatched cottage (Kinnoull) as you approach Nuney Green.

At a track near the entrance to Kinnoull turn right and go straight on at a junction. Just after a bungalow turn right on a footpath signed to Mapledurham. This takes you through Nuney Wood and after leaving the wood you continue forward by a field edge and a row of fine beeches and oaks to reach a lane.

Cross to another footpath which takes you past Whittles Farm. Before long, a stile on the right gives access to sheep pasture, with a lovely view of Bottom Wood and Colins End. Keep left beside a line of trees along the edge of the pasture, soon descending to join the bridleway you used near the start of the walk. Turn left to return to Mapledurham House. Mapledurham village is close by but for information about it please see walk 10.

Nuney Green

Walk 10: Reading to Pangbourne

Start: Reading Station; grid reference 715738.

Finish: Pangbourne Station; grid reference 633766.

Summary: This enjoyable linear walk begins and ends in Berkshire, but most of it is in Oxfordshire, in peaceful country between the Chilterns and the Thames, with the delightful village of Mapledurham close to the halfway point. Much of the walk is on hard-surfaced tracks and lanes and there are no stiles.

Length: 7 miles/11.2km.

Maps: OS Landranger 175, OS Explorer 171.

Buses/coaches: Local and national operators provide frequent services to Reading; links between Reading and Pangbourne are operated by Reading Buses 105/106, Monday to Saturday; also Weavaway Travel X48 (Ridgeway Explorer)Wantage to Reading via Pangbourne, Sundays/BHMs from April to October.

Trains: Frequent daily services operate to Reading from all over the country; Thames Trains operates daily services between Oxford and Paddington via Reading and Pangbourne.

Parking: Public car parks in Reading or Pangbourne.

The Tea Shop

The Coffee Pot, 12 High Street, Pangbourne.

This cosy, welcoming café is Italian-run and offers prompt and friendly service. Hot meals are served all day and a comprehensive choice is provided, including substantial breakfasts, omelettes, lasagne (including a veggie version), moussaka, scampi, jackets, chilli con carne and soup. Salads and sandwiches are freshly made to order and an alluring range of home-made cakes and scones is on offer. There are ice creams too, and a good choice of drinks, with tea coming in generous pots. Vegetarians will have no trouble finding something suitable; vegetable stock is used for soups and eggs are free-range. There are both smoking and no-smoking tables. Dogs are not allowed and walkers are asked to remove muddy boots on entry.

Open: 9.00am-5.30pm Monday, Wednesday, Thursday, Friday, Saturday; 10.00am-6.00pm Sunday. Closed Christmas week. Telephone: 0118 9843207.

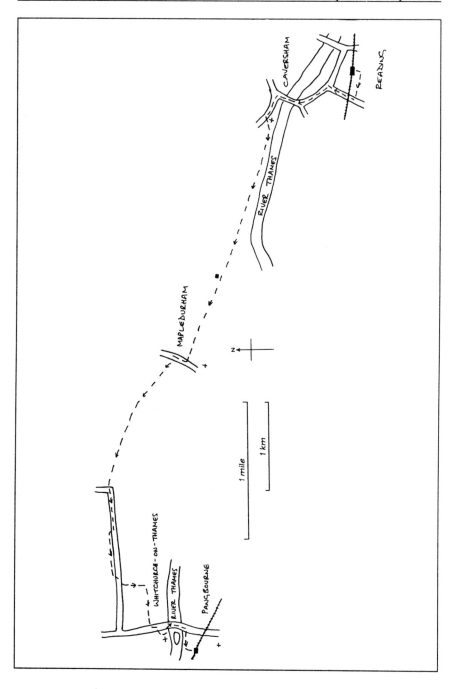

Reading

Established by the Saxons on the River Kennet, a tributary of the Thames, Reading came to prominence after the foundation of a Benedictine abbey in 1121 by Henry I. The burgeoning town prospered from wool trading and cloth manufacture and was given a considerable boost in the 19th century when it was chosen for an important junction on the Great Western Railway. Before that, in 1826, The Huntley & Palmer Biscuit Company had been established in the town and its factory became the biggest of its kind in the world, employing thousands of local people. That factory has now closed but Reading continues to grow, with new office blocks seeming to appear every week. Reading generally gets a bad press and certainly no one could call it beautiful. It does, however, have plenty of interest, especially for those appreciative of Victorian municipal architecture. On the other hand, it's remarkably easy to escape from on foot, largely because of the way it has focussed on the Kennet and turned its back on the Thames, which provides the ideal exit.

The Walk

Leave Reading Station by the main entrance and turn right through the bus station then straight on at the junction with Tudor Road. Turn right on Caversham Road, cross at the pelican crossing opposite the Royal Mail building and go over Caversham Bridge.

Continue to a junction and turn left on Church Road. Go through St Peter's Churchyard to emerge on The Warren, a leafy residential street. Turn left and walk past grand houses whose gardens border the Thames. As the houses thin out and the lane becomes a bridleway you enter Oxfordshire.

Just keep straight on at all junctions to arrive at Mapledurham, a tiny community consisting of one street of beautiful 17th-century brick and flint cottages and almshouses, a church and majestic Mapledurham House, set in its own extensive grounds. After the Conquest there were two manors of Mapledurham (not united until 1582) and the largest was held by the Bardolph family who built the present church in the 13th century. In 1440 their estate was bought by the Blount family, whose descendants still live at Mapledurham House. In the 1860s the vicar of the church was Edward Coleridge, a nephew of the poet Samuel Taylor Coleridge. The church was used in the film *The Eagle has Landed* in 1971.

Turn right up the lane until you reach the White House where you join a bridleway signed to Whitchurch. The hedged track runs through the Hardwick Estate below rolling downland. At a junction bear left to proceed in the same direction, passing flamboyant neo-Tudor stables at Hardwick Stud Farm. Keep straight on at a road junction, ignoring a footpath on the left. Pass Bozedown Vineyard, where wine-tasting is available at the shop. After this a path, Jubilee Walk, runs parallel with the road on top of a bank.

When you reach Primrose Hill cross to a footpath opposite which leads to a school where you turn right along Eastfield Lane. This takes you to the main road at Whitchurch. Turn left and cross over to join the Thames Path, which leads through the churchyard, past an old mill and over the toll bridge (pedestrians go free) into Pangbourne, one of the earliest crossing places on the Thames. If you're going direct to the station take a footpath on the right just after the Boathouse Surgery, walking past a lock and weir before emerging close to the station. If you're going to the Coffee Pot just keep forward into the village and you can't miss it. Pangbourne is a pleasant little place which was a popular riverside resort in Edwardian days. Kenneth Grahame, author of *Wind in the Willows*, lived at Church Cottage until his death in 1932.

The River Thames at Reading, from Caversham Bridge

Walk 11: Shiplake

Start/finish:	Shiplake Station; grid ref 776797.
Summary:	An effortless circular walk on exceptionally well-defined footpaths. It combines a stretch of the Thames Path with farmland and woodland paths on the edge of the Chilterns and provides the opportunity to visit the lovely village of Sonning, just across the river in Berkshire.
Length:	8 miles/12.8km.
Maps:	OS Landranger 175, OS Explorer 171.
Buses/coaches:	Reading Buses 127 Reading to Maidenhead via Sonning, Monday to Saturday; 125 Reading to Twyford via Sonning, Sunday; Reading Buses/Wycombe Bus Company 328/329/330 Reading to High Wycombe via Shiplake and Sonning, daily.
Trains:	Thames Trains Reading to Henley via Shiplake, daily.
Parking:	Shiplake Station.

The Tea Shop

The Tea Cosy, 6 High Street, Sonning on Thames.

Also the village store, this is a cosy and friendly place where you eat in a beamed room with a wood-burning stove, an old oak dresser and a comfy sofa. Displays of old plates and copper kettles add to the ambience. The Tea Cosy is open for morning coffee, lunch and afternoon tea, with home-made cakes and light meals available all day. Snacks on toast, jacket potatoes, omelettes and sandwiches are all served with side salad and home-made soups come in an imaginative range. An excellent range of daily specials includes plenty of vegetarian choices such as chickpea hotpot, wheat and walnut casserole and vegetable pasta bake. There are plenty of traditional standbys including ploughman's lunches, English breakfasts, crumpets, teacakes, muffins, scones and clotted cream teas, as well as desserts, ice creams and the usual range of hot and cold drinks. Smokers are welcome at outside tables and dogs are welcome outside too.

Open: 10.00am-5.00pm daily; closed Mondays November-February. The shop is open 7.00am-5.30pm daily. Telephone: 01889 9698178.

Shiplake

There are two Shiplakes – the old village, and Lower Shiplake, which is further north, much larger and Victorian/Edwardian in style, having grown up around the railway station. It remains very much a commuter settlement today. Lower Shiplake was the first English home of the writer George Orwell, whose parents chose a house here after returning from India. They lived at Roselawn on Station Road, before moving to Henley a few years later.

Shiplake Lock

The Walk

Leave the station and immediately join the Thames Path, turning left on Station Road to a crossroads and then left on Mill Road. Keep left at a junction with New Road and at the entrance to Lashbrook House Nursing Home turn left then shortly right over a stile to follow the Thames Path across fields to Mill House. Turn right, then left towards Shiplake Lock. Just before the lock the path turns right to run

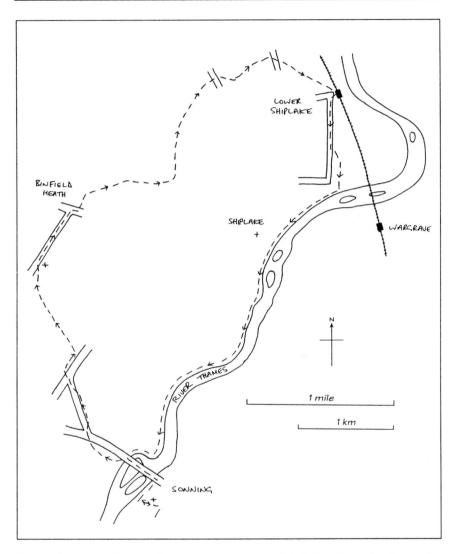

through riverside meadows. As you pass Shiplake Church a branching path provides the opportunity to visit it. Alfred, Lord Tennyson, was married in this church in 1850.

Eventually you come to Sonning Bridge where you cross the Thames into Berkshire. Turn right, still on the Thames Path, until a sign directs you left to the Tea Cosy. Go through the churchyard and forward to the High Street.

Sonning is a beautiful village, full of mellow brick Georgian houses and cottages. It's hard to believe that Reading is only a couple of miles away; hard to believe too, that this was a Saxon bishopric before the see was moved to Salisbury. There is an interesting church and some renowned pubs and restaurants, including the Bull, recommended by Jerome K Jerome in *Three Men in a Boat*.

Return over the bridge into Oxfordshire and keep straight on past The Mill (a theatre and restaurant). When you draw level with the French Horn turn left on a footpath which takes you past Furleigh Cottages. At a T-junction turn left, and soon right by a house called Long Gardens. At the next junction go straight on along a "no through road" to reach the B478. Cross with care and go straight on along the lane opposite. This is surprisingly busy but soon you can join a footpath on the right which runs parallel with the lane for a while. When forced to rejoin the lane keep on in the same direction to meet the A4155 and cross with care to join a permissive field-edge path opposite, turning right on it. At the end of the path a left turn takes you onto a gently rising tree-lined bridleway. At a fork continue along the bridleway.

Reaching the road at Binfield Heath turn right. When you reach a T-junction by the post office cross the road and turn right, then left just after a phone box. Go straight on at a junction by Applethwaite Cottage and turn right along a track at the next junction, by Pond House.

Coming eventually to a T-junction turn left on a footpath, lined with bluebells in spring. Walk through Hailey Woods and Shiplake Woods and across fields to a lane. Turn right and soon cross a road, continuing along a bridleway opposite between Little Beeches and Cray House. Cross another road to join a fenced footpath opposite, which runs diagonally to emerge on a residential lane at Shiplake. Walk on down the lane to reach Station Road and turn left to the station.

Walk 12: Henley

Start/finish: Market Place, Henley-on-Thames; grid reference 760826.

Summary: Beautiful beechwoods and a lovely stretch of the River Thames are the main ingredients of this easy circular walk which also allows you to explore one of England's most famous small towns.

Length: 6 miles/9.6km.

Maps: OS Landranger 175, OS Explorer 171.

Buses/coaches: Stagecoach Oxford X39 Oxford to Heathrow via Henley, daily; Reading Buses/Wycombe Bus Company 328/329/330/331 Reading to High Wycombe via Henley, daily; local services operated by Chiltern Queens.

Trains: Thames Trains operates daily services from Reading/Twyford with excellent connections to Oxford and London Paddington.

Parking: Public car parks in Henley.

The Tea Shop

Asquith's Tea Shop, 2-4 New Street, Henley.

On the corner of New Street and Bell Street stands a medieval building, at least 550 years old, the ground floor of which is inhabited by hundreds of teddy bears looking for new owners. This is Asquith's Teddy Bear Shop and upstairs the theme continues in the oak-beamed tea rooms with teddy table mats and teddy paintings on the walls. This is a traditional tea room where morning coffee, lunch and afternoon tea are served. The lunch menu consists of soup of the day, dish of the day, a vegetarian special, jacket potatoes, puddings, wine and coffee. The dish of the day can be anything from curry to seafood. At other times of day you can choose from a range of delicious home-made cakes, scones, tea cakes etc. Vegetarians, and even vegans, are catered for and all food is freshly cooked. Neither smoking nor dogs are permitted.

Open: 9.00am-5.30pm Monday to Saturday; 11.00am-6.00pm Sunday.

Henley

Henley is an attractive town beautifully situated on the Thames. It grew from a small river port into an important coaching centre and there are many former coaching inns among the splendid 16th-, 17th- and 18th-century buildings which throng its streets. The Red Lion, for instance, has played host to a diverse clientele, including Charles I, Prince Rupert, the Prince Regent, the Duke of Wellington, Dr Johnson and Boswell. The 13th-century church was much restored by the Victorians but is still an imposing sight with its tall flint-and-stone chequered tower overlooking the river. The nearby bridge is one of the finest in Oxfordshire, embellished with carvings of Father Thames and Isis. However, Henley is world-famous not for its buildings but for the Royal Regatta, which was started in 1839 and takes place in the first week of July. The course, which was used for the first Oxford and Cambridge boat race, runs from the bridge to Temple Island. The whole town is in holiday mood while the regatta lasts, and it is now followed by the increasingly popular Henley Festival, a riverside arts and music event. July is definitely the best time to enjoy this colourful town which, unlike so many in Britain, really does make the most of its river.

Henley

The Walk

From the Market Place turn right on Duke Street, right again on
Greys Road, left on Church Street, straight on past the church and a
school and on along Vicarage Road. Go straight on at the junction
with St Mark's Road and just after a postbox turn right on a footpath.
Follow it across St Andrew's Road and across another street onto
Cromwell Road. Continue along here until you can leave it on the
right for another footpath, soon crossing another street and continuing forward. Reaching a lane, turn left; this is Peppard Lane.

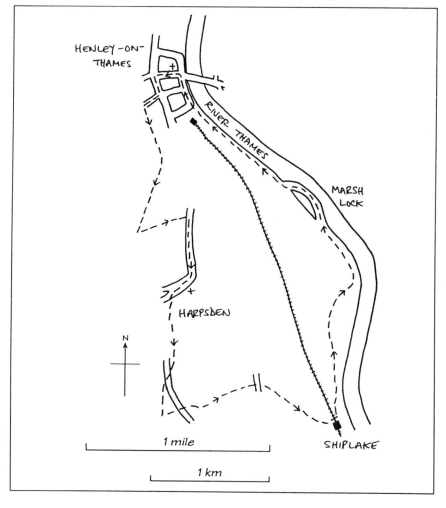

On arriving at a junction with Harpsden Way, turn right and descend towards Harpsden. Turn right to pass 16th-century Harpsden Court and 12th-century St Margaret's Church. Just before a gate into a cemetery turn left onto a narrow path which descends through lovely Harpsden Wood to a point where you join a road. Keep straight on in the same direction and, when the road bends left, leave it to join another footpath.

When you reach another road turn left and go straight on at the junction ahead, along a bridleway between Little Beeches and Cray House. Cross another road to join a fenced footpath opposite, which runs diagonally to emerge on a residential lane at Shiplake. Walk on down the lane to reach Station Road and turn left. Walk over the level crossing by Shiplake Station, then turn left on the Thames Path. It's now just a question of following the waymarked route past Bolney Court and across fields to the river then downstream to Henley. This final section of the walk includes the crossing of two long wooden bridges at Marsh Lock before you pass the recently opened (late 1998) River and Rowing Museum, which is well worth a visit.

Walk 13: Nettlebed to Henley

Start:	Nettlebed Common; grid reference 702868.
Finish:	Market Place, Henley-on-Thames; grid reference 760826.
Summary:	Woodland and "horsiculture" are the main features of this delightful and very easy linear walk in typical Chilterns country, and the charming town of Henley makes an ideal finishing point. If you have a dog make sure it is not allowed to run free because the only unpleasant thing about this walk is the occurrence of signs warning of "vermin control". This presumably means that poisoned bait is put down, an indiscriminate method of killing which makes no distinction between species.
Length:	5 miles/8km.
Maps:	OS Landranger 175, OS Explorer 171.
Buses/coaches:	Stagecoach Oxford X39 Oxford to Heathrow via Nettlebed and Henley, daily; for details of other services to Henley see walk 12.
Trains:	Thames Trains operates daily services to Henley from Reading/Twyford with excellent connections to Oxford and London Paddington.
Parking:	Public car parks in Henley; roadside parking at Nettlebed.

The Tea Shop

Crispins Tea Rooms, Bridge House, 52 Hart Street, Henley-on-Thames.

Established in 1971, Crispins is still under the original ownership. Occupying a fine Georgian house close to the river, it's decorated in traditional style with potted palms, a woodburning stove, gilt-framed mirrors and café curtains providing an attractive setting in which to enjoy your choice from a comprehensive menu. All food is freshly prepared and, as you would expect in quintessentially English Henley, there are cream teas, scones, tea cakes, home-made cakes and apple pie. There is a good range of more substantial meals, including sandwiches, toasted sandwiches, soup, fish dishes, quiche with salad, snacks on toast, omelettes and various daily specials such as lasagne. There are plenty of puddings and desserts to choose from and the drinks menu includes speciality and herb teas, as well as all the usual choices. Vegetarians are catered for and the premises are non-smoking. Dogs are welcome if clean and well-behaved.

Open: 1.00pm-7.30pm weekdays (except Mondays); 10.00am-7.30pm weekends and bank holidays.

Nettlebed

This compact little community is surrounded by beautiful beechwoods but suffers from the traffic which thunders incessantly along the main street, which just happens to be the A4130. But it's worth taking a look round before you start the walk because there are some attractive 18th-century brick houses in characteristic Chilterns style and the 19th-century church has windows by John Piper. Near the bus stop there is an old brick kiln, recalling an industry which employed local people for 500 years or more.

Horses near Nettlebed

The Walk

Alight from the bus at Nettlebed Common, at the south end of Nettlebed, and walk towards Henley, soon turning right beside the B481. Woodland, predominantly beech, borders the road on both sides. Go straight on at a junction, passing the entrance to Joyce Grove. This is a Sue Ryder home now, but was previously the home of Ian Fleming, creator of James Bond.

Very soon after this, turn left on a bridleway, leaving the road for the peace of the woodland. Go quietly and you may see one of the Muntjac deer which frequent these woods. Ignore all branching paths, staying on the main track, which eventually curves to the left, passing to the right of a paddock to reach a T-junction where you turn left, still by the paddock. At the next junction turn right on a rhododendron-lined path which climbs slightly and soon curves left, passing Westleaze Cottage before continuing between fields.

At a crosstracks go straight on towards Bromsden Farm. Pass some magnificent timber barns then bear slightly to the right to find a bridleway sign. This directs you into woodland, with the path curving to the left and then to the right before descending towards the valley floor. Go straight on at two crosstracks, passing a wood belonging to the National Trust, which is open to the public if you wish to explore it. It's part of the Greys Court estate.

At a lane turn left, and quite soon you'll see a footpath on the left which leads to Greys Court, a worthwhile detour. Greys Court is a picturesque Tudor mansion built by a member of the Knollys family in the 16th century. It stands on the site of a fortified manor house originally built in the 14th century by Walter de Grey, Archbishop of York. Some of de Grey's house still survives and there are interesting outbuildings, beautiful walled gardens and a maze created by Lady Brunner, whose family came to Greys in the 1930s. The house now belongs to the National Trust and is open from April to September, though not every day.

Continuing along the lane to reach a junction, cross over before turning right on a path beside the road. When it rejoins the road at Greys Green turn left on another path, which winds past woodland until a stile gives access to pasture. Keep forward along its right-hand edge and thereafter just straight on, ignoring all branching paths as you follow a well-trodden path along a valley. At a crosspaths carry straight on and, all too soon, you'll reach the first

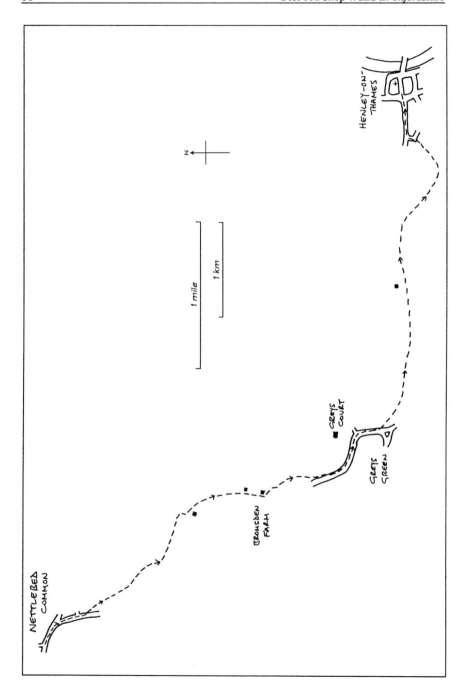

houses on the edge of Henley. Just keep forward in the same direction then, when you come to Paradise Road, turn left, then right down Gravel Hill into Henley.

Henley

For information about Henley please see walk 12.

Walk 14: Chalgrove to Watlington

Start: High Street, Chalgrove; grid reference 637968.

Finish: High Street, Watlington; grid reference 689946.

Summary: A varied linear walk on the edge of the Chilterns which includes picturesque villages, the unspoilt small town of Watlington and a fine stretch of the Ridgeway, culminating in Watlington Hill, famous for good views, wild flowers and yew trees. Though a fairly long walk, it is not at all strenuous.

Length: 9 miles/14.5km.

Maps: OS Landranger 164 and 165 or 174, OS Explorer 171.

Buses/coaches: Stagecoach Oxford 101 Oxford to Lewknor via Chalgrove and Watlington, Monday to Saturday; 103 Oxford to Chalgrove, Monday to Saturday; Yellow Bus M1 Reading to High Wycombe via Watlington, Monday to Saturday; some other local services are available and a few connections with Goring & Streatley Station (via Thames Travel 132) and with the Oxford Tube (24-hour coach service between Oxford and London) at Lewknor via bus 101.

Trains: Nearest stations are Cholsey or Henley, but Didcot, Goring & Streatley and Oxford are not much further and may be more convenient.

Parking: Public car park in Watlington or roadside parking in Chalgrove.

The Tea Shop

Copyhold Pantry, 18 High Street, Watlington.

Established in 1981, originally as a farm shop, Copyhold Pantry has gained a reputation for its hand-made gourmet dishes made from fresh, natural ingredients. These are packed in various portion sizes and then frozen, offering customers a far superior version of the sort of ready-made meals which are now so popular in supermarkets. The new shop in Watlington also has a coffee shop and provides congenial surroundings in which to select from a fairly small but enormously appetising range of goodies. There are freshly prepared and unusually well-filled sandwiches, a variety of quiches, imaginative and delicious soups such as carrot and orange, vegetable samosas, bacon butties and a choice of devastating cakes. Many of the items are suitable for vegetarians. The usual selection of drinks is on offer and everything is available to take away, at lower prices than eating in. Dogs are not permitted and there is no smoking.

Open 9.00am-5.00pm Monday to Saturday, except Wednesday when it closes at 2.00pm. Telephone: 01491 614820

Chalgrove

This large, mainly modern village looks uninteresting at first sight, but there are several very attractive older houses still surviving and a fine 14th-century church. The chancel is decorated with medieval wall paintings but you may find the church door locked – try Ashworth's Newsagent on High Street for the key. In 1643 the Battle of Chalgrove Field (to the north of the village) was a victory for the Royalists under Prince Rupert, and resulted in the death of the great Parliamentary commander John Hampden, who is remembered by a monument at the battle site.

Chalgrove

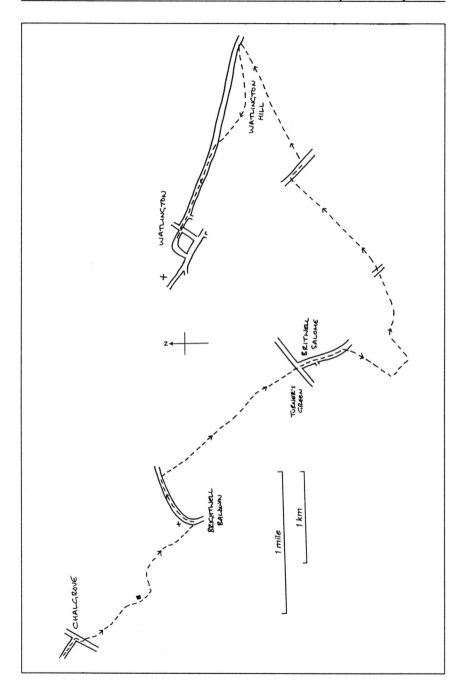

The Walk

Alight from the bus on High Street and walk towards Watlington. (If you want to visit the church, take either Church Lane or Baronshurst Drive). At a junction turn right on Berrick Road and shortly cross to join a footpath on the left signed to Brightwell Baldwin. Follow the left-hand edge of a paddock to a stile and turn left on a surfaced bridleway.

Walk past fields, woods and plantations, then past a farm, soon after which the bridleway makes a sharp left turn. When you come to a junction at a corner of a wood keep straight on and the same at all subsequent junctions. When you reach a road turn left into Brightwell Baldwin, which consists of a 14th-century church, a pub and a few houses. The church is particularly interesting. On the north wall of the nave is a brass memorial to John ye Smyth who died in 1371. The inscription is believed to be the first written in English. The parish chest features a painting of St George, which probably dates from the 14th century, and the Cottesmore brasses are notable for their detailed portrayal of 15th-century dress. A mat in the porch protects a memorial to Stephen Rumbold who died in 1687 at the age of 105.

Walk through the village until you find a bridleway signed to Britwell Salome on the right. This lovely green lane (Turner's Green Lane) heads directly towards the Chilterns, with Watlington Hill prominent from this angle. At a road junction by the twin communities of Turner's Green and Britwell Salome carry straight on along the lane opposite, by a pub. Pass through the village and take the second right, a bridleway which leads past Britwell Salome House. Soon after passing the house turn sharp left on a footpath, heading towards steep Icknield Bank. At a junction turn left on a bridleway, the Swan's Way. At the next junction go forward on the Ridgeway (also still the Swan's Way and the Icknield Way, too).

Carry straight on at a road junction, with a field of free-range pigs on your left, and straight on again at the next two junctions. When you reach a road turn right and shortly cross to take a track on the left, soon forking left on a path which climbs up Watlington Hill. When you reach a road turn left to find a path giving access to the hill. Much of Watlington Hill belongs to the National Trust and there is open access for the public. It's an excellent site for chalk-loving wild flowers and the butterflies which feed on them. It also has lovely beechwoods, areas of scrub and some yew woodland, which is unusual in the Chilterns. Having explored the hill, follow the main path down to a road and keep straight on into Watlington.

Watlington

Though this is officially a town, it must be one of the smallest in the country, and its narrow winding streets are packed with lovely 17th- and 18th-century houses and a charming town hall of 1664, which has also served as a grammar school and a covered market. There was a Norman castle once but all traces of it have disappeared. The church is hidden away on the western edge of the little town but worth searching out to admire the gargoyles and other carvings.

Walk 15: Banbury

Start/finish: Banbury Bus Station; grid reference 458407.

Summary: An enjoyable circular walk in gently rolling farmland, linking a bustling market town with a gorgeous rural village. One thing that they both have in common is the warm ironstone used in their construction, a characteristic feature of Oxfordshire's Cherwell Valley, and imbued with such a deep golden glow that it seems almost to warm the air on cold winter days.

Length: 10 miles/16km.

Maps: OS Landranger 151, OS Pathfinders 1022 and 1045, OS Explorer 191 (publication expected late 1999).

Buses/coaches: Stagecoach Midland Red X59 Oxford to Banbury, Monday to Saturday; 488/489 Chipping Norton to Banbury, Monday to Saturday; 499 Aynho to Banbury, Monday to Saturday; 500/508 Brackley to Banbury, Monday to Saturday; Newmark Coaches 270 Stratford to Banbury, Monday to Saturday; also a variety of other local services.

Trains: Thames Trains and Virgin Trains operate frequent services to Banbury.

Parking: Public car parks in Banbury.

The Tea Shop

Geranium Tea Shoppe, 13 White Lion Walk, Banbury.

You might have to search a bit to find this one, for White Lion Walk is one of a charming jumble of alleys and narrow streets connecting High Street with Market Place and Horse Fair. Once you've found it you're assured of a friendly welcome and prompt service. Choose from a wide range of light meals, including snacks on toast, quiche, ploughman's, home-made soup, cottage pie, pasties, baked potatoes, sandwiches and salads. Tea-time treats include crumpets, scones, tea cakes, pastries and cakes. The owner, Mrs Steel, says that this is the only tea shop in town which makes its own Banbury cakes (spiced, fruity cakes made in Banbury since Tudor times). A choice of sweets and ice creams is also available, and drinks include tea, coffee, elderflower pressé, fruit juices and a range of fruit-flavoured sparkling drinks. Vegetarians will find something suitable but should ask for details if unsure. Dogs are welcome and smoking is permitted. In summer, there are tables outside.

Open: 9.30am-4.00pm daily. Telephone: 01295 257966.

Banbury

The home of Europe's largest cattle market, Banbury was founded long ago next to a crossing point of the River Cherwell, from which radiated many of the main highways linking the Midlands with Oxford and London. In the Middle Ages the wool trade brought great prosperity and much of the medieval street pattern survives, though there are few medieval buildings and Banbury Cross, of nursery rhyme fame, was destroyed by the Puritans. Today, Banbury is a busy place and a major redevelopment has just begun in the town centre, but there are still many attractive buildings lining its streets and it's well worth setting aside half a day to explore the town.

The Walk

Walk through the bus station to join the towpath of the Oxford Canal and turn left to head north. You're now on the Oxford Canal Walk, which links Oxford to Coventry, and the Grand Union Canal Walk to the Thames Path. The Oxford Canal, completed in 1790, was engineered by James Brindley to a "contour" specification, meaning it winds picturesquely around hills, avoiding the need for cuttings and embankments.

Continue for about a mile (1.6km) on the towpath, past Spiceball Country Park, an industrial estate and the A423 (Southam Road) until a footbridge allows you to cross the canal. Turn right beside the road then cross to join a footpath, created along the course of a former mineral railway which served ironstone quarries in the Wroxton area, linking them with the main GWR line. Follow the former railway past an industrial estate and through housing estates until you emerge on the Warwick Road.

Turn left, then soon right on Stratford Road, heading towards Drayton. Very soon you can join a footpath on the right, which goes diagonally left across a field to Drayton. Turn right along the road until you can join a footpath on the left, which heads directly across fields towards Wroxton. When you reach the village, turn left on Church Street, which bends to the right after passing the church and leads to the village centre.

Wroxton is a beautiful village packed with delightful ironstone cottages, many of them thatched. A left turn leads into the grounds of Wroxton College, a grand Elizabethan house built on the site of an Augustinian monastery. The grounds are embellished with lakes, trees and some curious follies, and are open to the public. You're free to explore as you wish, but to continue the walk take the footpath which closely skirts a garden near the entrance. The path leads into a field where there is a choice of two paths. Take the left-hand one, which leads downhill to pass between two pools, before climb-

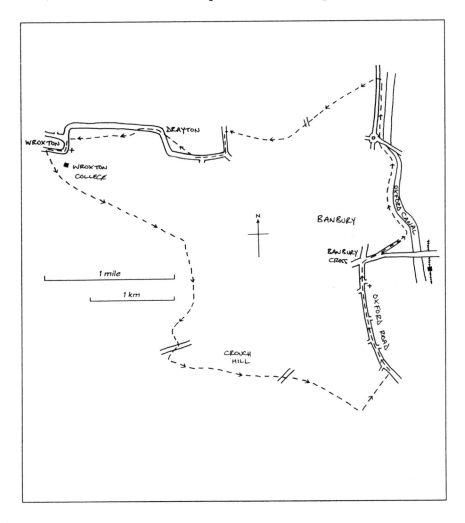

Guidepost at Wroxton

ing uphill to pass an obelisk. Continue in the same direction, aiming for a ruined arch (a folly) in woodland on top of the next ridge.

After crossing a stone footbridge, head up the slope to the folly then walk towards Banbury to intercept a wide cross-track. Turn right and follow it all the way to Broughton Road. Just before you reach the road there is an area of old pasture known as the Bretch, and the scant remains of Giant's Cave, which is said by some to have been a secret entrance to a tunnel leading to Broughton Castle, nearly a mile (1.6km) away.

Cross the road to join a track known as the Salt Way, which is exactly what it once was – the main highway along which salt was transported from Droitwich to London. Follow it past Crouch Hill, across the Bloxham Road and on past playing fields until you see a track on the left, which leads to Oxford Road. Lined with fine buildings, this is the best approach to Banbury. Turn left towards the town. When you reach Banbury Cross (where a Victorian replica of the original cross stands) a right turn leads to the town centre and the bus and rail stations.

Walk 16: Cropredy

Start/finish: The Old Coal Wharf, Cropredy; grid reference 468465.

Summary: A short, easy and very enjoyable circular walk which links two lovely ironstone villages and includes a stretch of the Oxford Canal Walk.

Length: 3½ miles/5.6km.

Maps: OS Landranger 151, OS Pathfinder 1022 (Explorer due in 2000).

Buses/coaches: Stagecoach Midland Red 510 Banbury to Farnborough via Cropredy and Great Bourton, Monday to Saturday; Geoff Amos Coaches 4 Wormleighton to Banbury via Cropredy, Monday, Thursday and Saturday.

Trains: Nearest station is Banbury.

Parking: Parking is usually possible at the Old Coal Wharf but please ask first.

The Tea Shop

The Old Coal Wharf, The Plantation, Cropredy.

Warm and welcoming, and one of the most unusual venues in this book, the Old Coal Wharf also functions as the base for an arts and film society with regular film screenings and a very wide variety of other events. Housed in a refurbished 18th-century building with white-washed brick walls, the café has two large tables surrounded by comfortable cinema seats and there is an old-fashioned stove which not only ensures a cosy atmosphere but is also ideal for warming scones and pastries. Substantial continental breakfasts are served all day, and baked goods include scones, croissants, Danish pastries and tea cakes. Home-made soup is accompanied by toast and there is a daily special, which is always vegetarian. On Sundays a vegetarian roast lunch is served and places for this need to be reserved. Drinks include tea, coffee, hot chocolate, fruit juice, soft drinks and mineral water. Even though tea comes in generous pots to begin with, you will still be offered a free top-up. Dogs are welcome, and, although there is no smoking indoors, it is allowed outside where there is a covered canalside terrace.

Open: 12.00am-5.00pm Saturdays, Sundays and bank holidays; 1.00pm-5.00pm Monday to Thursday in summer. Closed January and February. Telephone: 01295 750878.

Cropredy

This is a lovely village, set in gentle farmland, with ironstone cottages clustered about the church, and both the Oxford Canal and the River Cherwell bordering it to the east. The mainly 14th-century church has many interesting memorials, including one to Labour minister Richard Crossman, who lived nearby until his death in 1974. It also contains a pre-Reformation brass lectern which is a great treasure. Local people hid it in the river to protect it from the Puritans, who went about the country destroying such things. It is said that when the danger had passed and they tried to fish it out it could not be found, and was only retrieved by chance 30 years later. Cropredy Bridge, spanning the Cherwell, was apparently already old when first recorded in 1312, and was the scene in 1644 of one of the fiercest battles of the Civil War, which resulted in victory for the Royalists, led by Charles I in person. The church contains a collection of relics from the battle, such as helmets and cannon balls.

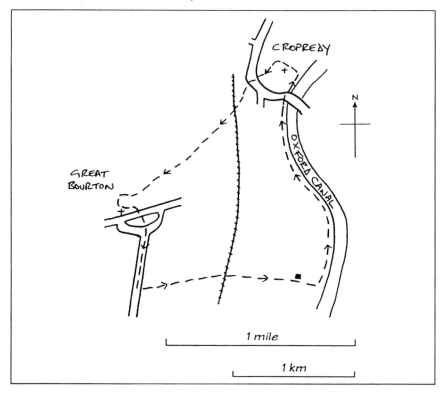

The Walk

Join the canal towpath beside the Old Coal Wharf, at bridge 153, and walk the short distance north to bridge 152. Leave the canal and walk up Red Lion Street then turn left along the edge of the church-yard and out through a gate in the corner. Go forward along Church Lane to the High Street and turn left to a green, then right. Cross the road and go into a cul-de-sac quaintly known as Cup and Saucer. Pass the shaft of a medieval preaching cross and turn left, then right at a sign for Great Bourton.

Walk past bungalows and turn left, then right, over two stiles and diagonally across a field (note that this path may be subject to diversion). Enter a belt of trees and turn left, over another stile and under

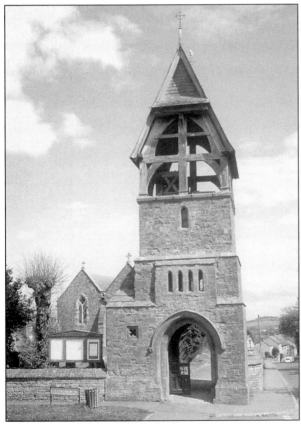

the railway to a gate on the left. Go diagonally across two arable fields then along the edge of the next field until a r a m s h a c k l e gate-cum-stile allows you to cross into another field. Follow the left-hand edge then over another stile into pasture with a very pronounced ridge and furrow pattern (from m e d i e v a l ploughing). The well-trodden path continues across more pasture and past a barn into one final field, at the

All Saints' Church, Great Bourton

top of which a stile gives access to a lane on the edge of Great Bourton. Turn right, then shortly left, passing some attractive old cottages, whose names indicate their former use: Nailers Cottage, Anvil Cottage and Forge Cottage. When you come to a T-junction turn left, and then right past Bell Cottage and the Bell Inn. On the left is All Saints' Church, with a curious lychgate-cum-belltower. The churchyard is quite beautiful in spring, smothered by a mass of primroses, lady's smock and celandine. Occupying a prominent knoll in the centre of the village, it overlooks some lovely houses.

Walk through the churchyard and down steps at the far end. Cross the main road and go up a footpath beside the village hall. Turn left at a T-junction and then right on Foxton Way towards Little Bourton. Immediately after Bourton Burial Ground turn left on a bridleway (Mill Lane) which leads down to the canal towpath, which provides an easy return route to Cropredy.

On the far side of the canal and the Cherwell is Williamscot House, a Tudor mansion where Charles I spent the night after the Battle of Cropredy Bridge.

Walk 17: Hornton

Start/finish: Upton House; grid reference 370457.

Summary: This effortless circular walk in pleasant farmland below Edge Hill ventures briefly into Warwickshire but the main focus is Hornton, one of those glorious ironstone villages which are the main asset of north Oxfordshire.

Length: 5 miles/8km.

Maps: OS Landranger 151, OS Pathfinder 1021 (Explorer due 2000).

Buses/coaches: Newmark Coaches 270 Stratford to Banbury via Upton House, Monday to Saturday; Stagecoach Midland Red 502 Kineton to Banbury via Ratley, Thursday and Saturday (connections to Kineton from Stratford and Leamington).

Trains: Nearest station is Banbury.

Parking: By the roadside; or you may use the National Trust car park when Upton House is open (assuming you intend to visit the house).

The Tea Shop

Upton House, near Banbury.

Two gleaming white Agas provide a focal point in this former kitchen, where wooden units, colourful tablecloths and fresh flowers offset the rather clinical white-tiled walls. There is seating for about three dozen people, but a pleasant sense of spaciousness is retained in this high-ceilinged room. Service is friendly and two high chairs are thoughtfully provided for small children. Choose from a range of set teas or from the superb variety of individual cakes, scones and teabreads on offer, or sample the special Upton shortbread. The scones and some of the cakes are suitable for vegetarians. The choice of drinks is good, including fruit teas and elderflower cordial. Ice creams are also available. Neither smoking nor dogs are permitted.

Open: 2.00pm-6.00pm Saturday to Wednesday, April to October (last teas at 5.30pm on weekdays in April and October). Telephone: 01295 670266.

Note: Upton House is a National Trust property so an entrance fee is payable, except by Trust members, even if you intend only to visit the tea room. Dogs are not permitted within the grounds.

Upton House

Built of mellow local stone, Upton is impressive and imposing, with a formal façade. The house dates from 1695 and contains an outstanding collection of paintings, tapestries, porcelain, Chelsea figures and 18th-century furniture. The garden is also of great interest, with magnificent herbaceous borders, terraces, a kitchen garden, a water garden and ornamental pools.

The Walk

From the main entrance turn right alongside the road and take the third left, a lane signposted to Hornton. Before long a footpath (don't join it) crosses the road – this marks the point at which you leave Warwickshire for Oxfordshire. Not long after you've passed Varney's Garage join a footpath on the right at a stile. Go diagonally left across a field grazed by horses, to a stile about halfway along the far hedge. Cross a farm track and go over another stile into a field of

Hornton

sheep and horses. Go straight ahead, descending towards the far hedge, over another stile and forward by a hedge of mature hawthorn and maple, walking at the bottom of a tree-covered bank.

As a stream comes in from the right, you'll see a stile on the left. Cross over and continue in much the same direction through a long, narrow field enclosed by tall hedges, with marshland and willow trees on your right. When the hedge on your left comes to an end and the field widens out bear left towards the far hedge. After going through an open gateway continue on the obvious path across a large area of pastureland towards Hornton. A stile soon gives access to a green lane which leads into the village centre.

The village is built of locally quarried stone, known in the area as gingerbread stone because of its colour, but known more widely as Hornton stone. It has been used in Canterbury Cathedral and St Paul's, in Oxford and Cambridge colleges and throughout the world. Hornton Church was built of it in the 12th century. Dedicated to St

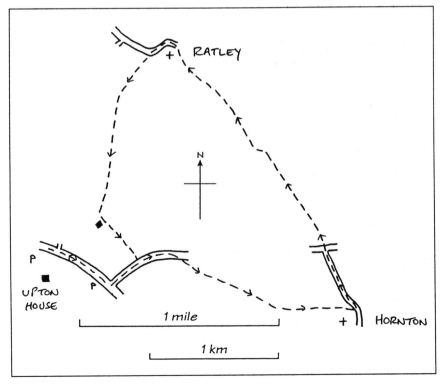

John the Baptist, the church is noted for its wall paintings which date from the 14th century and include a depiction of the Black Prince as St George. There is also a doom painting (judgment day) which may be from the 12th or 13th century.

Having explored the village, follow the main street north and keep going to reach a junction with another lane. Cross to a bridleway opposite and follow it towards Ratley. It descends Bush Hill to cross Sor Brook, the boundary between Oxfordshire and Warwickshire, then climbs out of the valley to enter the village of Ratley. Like its neighbour, this is another idyllic place of gingerbread stone. Beautiful cottages and farmhouses cluster round a 13th-century church and a pub which claims to have been established in 1098.

Follow the lane through the village, leaving the church behind on your left. As the lane bends, go left towards the entrance to Manor Farm. Approaching the gate, look for a stile on the right giving access to a field. Follow the right-hand field edge until it turns a corner. Go straight on instead, down a slope towards a stile. Walk diagonally left up the next field to the far corner, where there are two stiles. Climb the one on the left and go forward along a field edge. Cross another stile and go straight on along the edge of the next field, descending quite steeply into a valley and passing a derelict barn. After going through a gate, the path continues as a farm track across pasture before turning left over a stile and past a barn. Keep going along a tree-lined path, then over a broken stile into a field and forward to a lane. Turn right, then right again at the road, to return to Upton House.

Walk 18: The Rollrights

Start/finish: Hill Barn Farm, Great Rollright; grid reference 313316.

Summary: A very easy circular walk which includes two interesting villages and one of the foremost prehistoric monuments in England. The terrain is mostly level and stiles are few. Care is needed on a short stretch of road walking.

Length: 6 miles/9.6km.

Maps: OS Landranger 151, OS Explorer 191, OS Outdoor Leisure 45.

Buses/coaches: Stagecoach Oxford X50 Oxford to Stratford via Long Compton daily; Stagecoach Midland Red 488/489 Banbury to Chipping Norton via Great Rollright, Monday to Saturday; Barry's Coaches Moreton to Stratford via Long Compton, schooldays; Shipston Link from Shipston, Wednesdays and Fridays; the Shakespearean, a direct coach from London (Grosvenor Gardens) also operates, leaving at 9.00am and then running as the 10.50am X50 from Oxford.

Trains: Nearest station is Kingham.

Parking: You should normally be able to park at Hill Barn Farm, but should confirm this with the staff in the tea shop first. Alternative parking is available in a layby near the Rollrights (grid reference 296309).

The Tea Shop

Hill Barn Farm, Great Rollright, Chipping Norton.

This spacious restaurant, with fresh flowers on all the tables, and paintings by local artists on the walls, makes a very pleasant place for a break. There are far-reaching views to be enjoyed too, especially if you make use of the outdoor seating. All food is home-cooked on the premises and includes cakes, pastries, scones and a range of hot dishes such as pasta, grills, jackets, quiche and fish. There are plenty of vegetarian options and all soups are made with vegetable stock. The wide range of drinks includes many herbal and fruit teas. Guide dogs are welcome, and other dogs are permitted at the outside tables. There is no smoking. A well-stocked farm shop and garden centre adjoin the tea room.

Open: 10.00am-6.00pm May to September; 10.00am-5.00pm October to April. Telephone: 01608 684835.

The Rollrights

The main feature of the walk is the Rollright Stones, actually three separate prehistoric monuments. These comprise the King's Men, the Whispering Knights and the King Stone. Nobody really knows what these stones represent, or even how old they are, but the general concensus is that the Whispering Knights, actually four uprights and a fallen capstone, are the remains of a burial chamber constructed in the Neolithic period, maybe 4000 years ago. The King's Men, a circle of around 70 weather-worn uprights, and the King Stone, a solitary, intriguingly shaped stone taller than a man, are most likely Bronze Age, at least 3000 years old, and probably erected for ritual purposes.

The King Stone

The Rollrights seem to have always enjoyed considerable mystical significance, and in the Middle Ages peasants would chip pieces off to keep as charms against the Devil. Witches are reputed to have gathered here in Tudor times, and until comparatively recently local people used to meet at the stones once a year for dancing and drinking, perhaps continuing a long tradition of fertility rites. Today, battered and broken, the stones still cast a spell and New Age mystics dowse for ley lines and talk of fairies dancing round the King Stone, while strange sounds emanate from the Whispering Knights at a full moon.

The Walk

With your back to Hill Barn Farm, turn left along the road and keep straight on at a junction. A little further on, join a bridleway on the right, walking parallel with the road to a field corner then turning right. This brings you out at a crossroads where you turn left towards the church at Great Rollright. Walk through the churchyard and leave by the lychgate, turning right, then soon left down Tyte End. At the next junction turn right on Old Forge Road. At a junction by a green turn right on Hemplands to return to the crossroads encountered earlier. Turn left, and after about 600 yards/550m, join a footpath on the left (you may have to climb over a padlocked gate). A hedged green track gives way to a field-edge path and finally to a cross-field path but the route, effectively straight on, is never in doubt. Eventually, steps descend to a road. Cross and turn right for a few paces to find an unsigned footpath concealed by trees. Entering a field, the path is now waymarked and quite clear. A farm track is crossed and the path continues straight on (now part of the D'Arcy Dalton Way). After climbing a stile to a large field continue in the same direction. On your right you can see the Whispering Knights. The King's Men are further on, concealed by encircling pines.

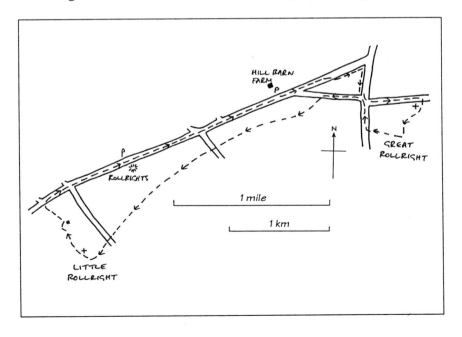

At a road cross to a footpath opposite, descending towards Little Rollright, which consists of little more than farm and church. On reaching a track turn right to visit St Philip's Church, a simple and atmospheric little building which contains some hugely impressive memorials, particularly the canopied marble chest tombs to members of the Dixon family.

Beyond the church join a footpath which climbs to a barn and then proceeds to a road. Turn right along the road, an ancient ridgeway route which offers fine views from its height of 710ft/216m, and forms the border between Oxfordshire and Warwickshire for the next mile or so. It is believed to have been part of one of Britain's earliest and most important tracks, the so-called Jurassic Way, leading along the limestone belt from the Humber to Dorset. Keep straight on at a crossroads to reach the Rollrights. First to be seen, on the Oxfordshire side of the road, is the stone circle known as the King's Men. A little further on, standing just inside Warwickshire, is the solitary King Stone, forever gazing north at the superb view. Further on again, in Oxfordshire, the Whispering Knights stand huddled in the middle of a field. When you reach another crossroads keep straight on to Hill Barn Farm.

Walk 19: Chipping Norton

Start/finish:	Market Place, Chipping Norton; grid reference 313271.
Summary:	An effortless circular walk on well-defined footpaths in pleasant, rolling countryside on the edge of a distinguished Cotswold town.
Length:	4½ miles/7.2km.
Maps:	OS Landranger 164, OS Explorer 191, OS Outdoor Leisure 45.
Buses/coaches:	Stagecoach Oxford X50 Oxford to Stratford via Chipping Norton, daily; 20/20A/20C Oxford to Chipping Norton, Monday to Saturday; Worth's Motor Services 69 Witney to Enstone via Chipping Norton, Monday to Saturday; 70 Oxford to Enstone via Chipping Norton, Monday to Saturday; Stagecoach Midland Red 488/489 Banbury to Chipping Norton, Monday to Saturday; there are numerous less frequent local services, and the Shakespearean, a direct coach from London (Grosvenor Gardens) also operates, leaving at 9.00am and then running as the 10.50am X50 from Oxford.
Trains:	Nearest station is Kingham.
Parking:	Public car park off New Street.

The Tea Shop

Annie's Country Pantry, 22 New Street, Chipping Norton.

Tucked away just outside the town centre, Annie's is an attractive stone building set back from the road next to a fascinating antique shop. With dried flowers decorating the interior walls, a traditional rug softening the floorboards and marble-topped tables partnered by bentwood chairs, the feel is warm and welcoming. There are tables outside too, in summer, and dogs are welcome at these. The choice of food is wide, including breakfasts, home-made soups, salads, ploughman's, omelettes, jackets, sandwiches, scones, cakes, cookies, teacakes, crumpets and traditional cream teas. There are daily specials and a vegetarian meal is listed most days. All soups are made with vegetable stock and the cakes are also suitable for veggies. The range of hot and cold drinks includes a marvellous choice of herbal and fruit teas. Smoking is permitted.

Open: 9.00am-5.00pm daily. Telephone: 01608 641100.

Chipping Norton

The highest town in Oxfordshire, Chippy, as locals call it, stands on the eastern side of a valley carved by the River Swere, a tributary of the Evenlode. By the time of the Domesday Survey in 1086 Norton was already a sizeable community, but the prefix, which means "market", was not acquired until the 13th century, when it was granted a charter for a weekly market and an annual fair. Chipping Norton soon grew rich on the proceeds of the wool trade and the wealth of the merchants is reflected in the fine buildings which throng the small town. Many were re-fronted in the 18th century, indicating that Chippy, thanks to its position on a major coaching route, continued to prosper after the decline of the wool trade.

Almshouses at Chipping Norton

The Walk

Leave Chipping Norton on New Street (the Worcester-bound A44) and walk as far as a recreation ground where two footpaths are indicated. Join the one signposted to Salford, pass to the left of a fenced play area and descend a sloping field. Cross the little River Swere and take the left-hand one of two footpaths, which runs up a field to a stile then crosses a track to another field before continuing gently uphill to a stile in the top left corner. Turn right through a hedge gap then immediately left along a field edge to the far corner. Enter a large arable field and enjoy the sudden panorama of Oxfordshire, Warwickshire and Gloucestershire which opens out ahead. Go straight on and very soon the village of Salford comes into view. Head towards the left-hand edge of it on a just-discernible path leading to a stile in a hedge. Go forward to another stile then along the other side of the hedge on a farm track. Walk through a farmyard (Village Farm) to enter Salford and go forward to a junction.

Turn left if you wish to visit St Mary's Church (Norman, but rebuilt in the 1850s by George Street, who retained some interesting details, such as the tympanum above the north door) but otherwise turn right on Cooks Lane. The houses along here are mostly new, submerging the original village, but a few old ones survive. At a major junction by a green turn right to find a signpost indicating a public right of way (actually a rupp - "road used as public path") to Over Norton.

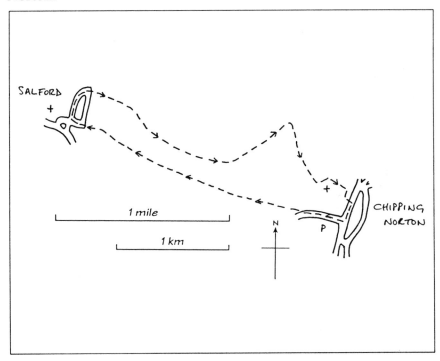

A surfaced lane at first, the right of way soon becomes a grassy track, easy to follow as it pursues a pleasant course between fields. As you approach Chipping Norton a footpath branches off to the right but ignore this and stay on the main track. As you come into line with the church you'll find another footpath on the right, running towards the town alongside a hedge. Very soon you need to cross (at a stile) to the other side of the hedge and the path is enclosed by two hedges now as it passes the dry moat and bumpy earthworks which reveal the position of Norton's long-gone Norman motte-and-bailey castle.

The path turns right to reach St Mary's Church, which is large and elegant, with a striking and most unusual hexagonal porch. Legend claims that this was built to commemorate the casting out of five devils from the church in 1302 by a priest named Henry of Winchcombe. He is said to have pursued them into the market place where he lost them in a flock of sheep.

The churchyard is pleasantly leafy and contains some interesting headstones, including one in memory of Phillis Humphreys, an itinerant rat catcher. Look for it close to the path on the south side of the church.

A choice of paths now awaits for your return to the town centre. If, for instance, you go up Church Street you will pass some charming 17th-century almshouses before you emerge at the junction of Spring Street and Market Street. Alternatively, a right turn along Diston Lane brings you back onto New Street, almost opposite Annie's Country Pantry.

Walk 20: Charlbury

Start/finish:	Charlbury Station; grid reference 352195.
Summary:	An easy circular walk on undemanding terrain in a pleasant and peaceful landscape. The footpaths, which include a stretch of the Oxfordshire Way, are well-maintained, have very few stiles and are easy to follow.
Length:	10 miles/16km.
Maps:	OS Landranger 164, OS Explorer 180.
Buses/coaches:	Worth's Motor Services 69 Enstone to Witney via Charlbury, Monday to Saturday; 70 Enstone to Oxford via Charlbury, Monday to Saturday.
Trains:	Thames Trains and Great Western operate daily services on the Cotswold Line.
Parking:	The car park at the station is meant for rail users, though there may sometimes be spaces available. There is a public car park in Charlbury.

The Tea Shop

The Coffeehouse Gallery, 11 Sheep Street, Charlbury.

11 Sheep Street is the oldest commercial building in Charlbury and has now been transformed by Peter Pelz into a delightful combination of coffee house and art gallery. Traditionally, a coffee house was a meeting place where people gathered to exchange views in a convivial atmosphere, and this sunny, spacious, friendly establishment lives up to the tradition. It's beautifully fitted out with restful lemon walls decorated with Peter's own vibrant paintings. Background music, plants and flowers, easy chairs and a newspaper-strewn coffee table by an old fireplace complete the ambience. The Gallery includes watercolours, etchings and tempera paintings and is housed in a separate room also used for meetings, film shows, recitals, readings and talks.

The food is equally impressive, with everything freshly prepared on the premises. The menu includes breakfast, morning coffee, lunch (soups, salads, ploughman's, omelettes, stuffed pancakes, falafel, fish and chicken dishes, cold meats, sandwiches, dish of the day, desserts), afternoon tea (cakes or scones with home-made jam and clotted cream) and a range of hot and cold all-day snacks. Vegetarian dishes are a particular speciality. As you would expect, there is a good range of coffees and teas, including fresh herbal teas, and a choice of other drinks too. Dogs are welcome but smokers are not. Open: 9.00am-5.30pm daily except Monday. Telephone: 01608 811414.

Charlbury

Charlbury nestles snugly in the Vale of Evenlode on the eastern edge of the Cotswolds. Far from any of the major roads which cross the wolds, it has retained its rural air and has not fallen victim to mass tourism. It was probably settled quite early in the Anglo-Saxon period and seems to have quietly flourished ever since, becoming a market town for a time and playing its part in the wool trade before achieving importance as a glove making centre.

For the walker, Charlbury's greatest asset is its position on the edge of what was once one of England's largest Royal Forests. Centred on Burford, Wychwood Forest stretched from Rollright to

The Oxfordshire Way at Charlbury

Woodstock, from the Windrush to the Cherwell. Every English king from Ethelred the Unready to James I is said to have hunted there. It was famous for its deer and subject to harsh Forest Law but the inhabitants of Burford enjoyed the right to hunt there on one day each year. As they also poached there on the remaining 364 days, it was often claimed that Oxford Gaol was built mainly to house Wychwood poachers. Unfortunately, Wychwood went the way of most other Royal Forests and by the 19th century the great parks of Ditchley, Blenheim, Cornbury and Eynsham had been carved out of it, while most of the rest had been cleared for farming. Only a small area of the Forest survives, ironically now just a part of the Cornbury Estate. Nevertheless, a new Wychwood Project has ambitious aims for the restoration of woodland cover.

The Walk

Leave Charlbury Station and walk towards the town. Turn right onto Church Lane, pass through the churchyard then turn right along another lane. After about 600 yards/550 metres turn right again, towards Cornbury Park. At North Lodge turn left to follow a footpath alongside the fence enclosing the park, where both red and fallow deer may be seen grazing beneath huge trees.

On reaching a trout fishery join a track but continue in the same direction, eventually reaching Charlbury Road. Cross to a footpath on the left and, after passing the entrance to a sewage works, follow the right-hand field edge until you reach another path close to the field corner. Walk down another field, ignoring a stile on the left, to find a green lane.

Turn left, walking through Topples Wood and eventually reaching a lane, Wilcote Riding. Turn left for a little way then join a footpath going diagonally left to the far corner of a field. As you pass the corner of a copse you're crossing the course of Akeman Street, a Roman road. At the far corner climb a stile to a lane, with beautiful Wilcote Manor on your right.

Turn left and keep straight on at two crossroads. A few paces after the second one join a footpath on the left, which runs alongside the River Evenlode. When the path eventually veers away from the river and arrives at a junction, go left through a pair of gates and across a field on a bridleway. Cross the Evenlode and follow a sunken lane up to Stonesfield, an attractive little place which once provided the stone roofing "slates" used all over the Cotswolds. The village church was built c1220 and contains some fine Early English work, particularly the chancel arch.

Turn left on High Street to reach Boot Street. Keep straight on, joining the Oxfordshire Way. The route is easily followed, but take care not to miss a left turn after a larch plantation. When you reach the edge of Charlbury cross a lane to a stone stile left of a bungalow. At the next road, cross to a path opposite which leads to a square of garages. Turn left to the main road, left again, then soon sharp right on Hixet Wood to reach the High Street. A left turn returns you to the station.

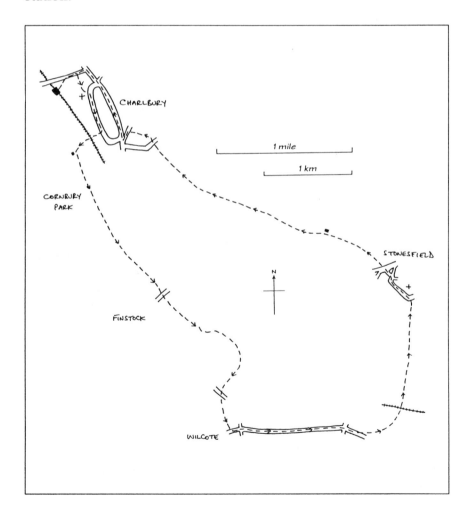

Walk 21: Kiddington

Start/finish: Kiddington crossroads; grid reference 410221.

Summary: An easy and delightful circular walk in undulating country on the edge of the Cotswolds. It includes farmland, woodland, plantation, the charming valley of the River Glyme and two attractive villages.

Length: 6 miles/9.6km.

Maps: OS Landranger 164, OS Pathfinders 1069 and 1092, OS Explorers 180 and 191 (publication of 191 is expected late 1999).

Buses/coaches: Stagecoach Oxford X50 Oxford to Stratford via Kiddington, daily; 20/20A/20C Oxford to Chipping Norton via Kiddington, Monday to Saturday; the Shakespearean, a direct coach from London (Grosvenor Gardens) also operates, leaving at 9.00am and then running as the 10.50am X50 from Oxford.

Trains: Nearest station is Charlbury.

Parking: Layby south of the crossroads.

The Tea Shop

Import Cottage Tea Rooms, Kiddington.

This attractive stone cottage functions as both tea room and shop, selling basketware, fabrics, ornaments and gifts. Home-made preserves are also on sale, ranging from four fruit marmalade to dragon's breath mustard. Teas are served in a low-ceilinged room, with cheerful yellow-painted walls and baskets piled high on the stone-flagged floor. Blue paintwork provides an attractive contrast to the yellow walls, while the table linen continues the blue and yellow theme. Choose from sandwiches, toast, tea cakes, cream teas, home-made cakes or Loseley ice cream. Sandwiches are freshly made to order and served with a salad garnish. Drinks include a range of teas, coffee, hot chocolate, herbal tea, milk, squash, Coca Cola and orange juice. No attempt is made to cater for vegetarians, though some items may be suitable. Children must be well-behaved and dogs are not permitted. There is no smoking.

Open: 11.00am-4.00pm daily; closed December, January and maybe February. Telephone: 01608 678303.

Kiddington

The village is just a scattering of cottages and farms around Kiddington Hall, which stands next to the parish church in the landscaped grounds of Kiddington Park. A few of the cottages stand by the crossroads near Import Cottage, in an area traditionally known as Over Kiddington, and the others are further north, closer to the hall, which was built in 1850 in Italianate style, replacing an earlier house on the same site. The River Glyme runs through Kiddington Park and has been dammed to form a couple of small lakes, apparently by Capability Brown who is said to have taken time off to work on Kiddington, and nearby Glympton, when he was employed on the creation of Blenheim Park, just down the road at Woodstock.

Kiddington church and dovecote

The Walk

Go down the lane signed to Ditchley, soon forking left at a junction on a bridleway which goes to Stonesfield. Continue past Grimsdyke Farm, between fields and then to the right of the oddly named Out Wood. At the eastern corner of the wood carry straight on across a field. At the corner of the field go forward through a bridle gate and then bear half-left across another field towards a line of conifers. When you reach it turn left, so that the trees are to your right, and keep straight on at a junction as you enter Kingswood Brake. Go quietly if you want to see the deer which inhabit this wood.

The gently undulating bridleway descends to cross a stream then goes forward to join a surfaced track on a bend. Take the right-hand option and go up to a road where you turn left on the grass verge. After a short distance turn left on another bridleway, soon descending into Ditchley Dell. Go through a gate and turn right along a field

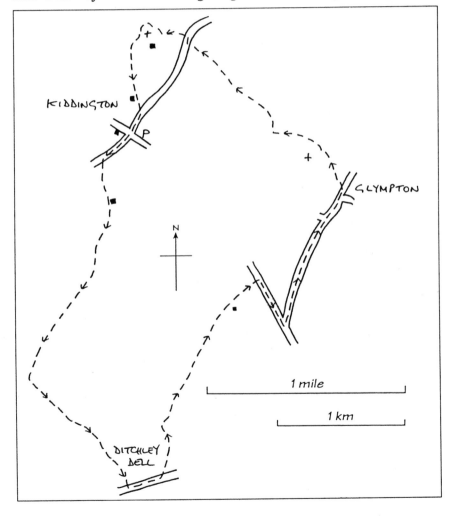

edge. The route is now obvious, through woodland and pasture, until you reach the road.

Turn right on the verge before crossing to take the first lane on the left, which leads into Glympton, an attractive village based around Glympton Park, an 18th-century mansion in parkland, also said to have been landscaped by Capability Brown.

Walk up the main street, passing the post office and a phone box, after which you turn left on a footpath. It runs across a field then descends steps to cross the driveway to Glympton Park. Ignore a stile ahead, continuing past it beside a line of massive trees, the River Glyme just below on the left. When a gate gives access to parkland carry on in the same direction alongside a fence until another gate opens into woodland, Long Meadow Copse. Turn right along its inner edge, with the Glyme snaking through the valley below.

Exiting from the wood, keep on along its outer edge and then along the edge of pasture. When the fence on your left turns a corner just continue in much the same direction on an obvious track. At the far side turn right along a rutted track and then keep to the left-hand edge of a field above a strip of woodland. When it comes to an end just keep straight on across the field. At the far side, join a track which bears right, descending to the lane at Kiddington.

Go along the lane opposite, shortly joining a path signed to Kiddington Church. This takes you along the driveway to Kiddington Hall until the drive forks. Go to the right, passing the church then turning left on to a track which skirts the churchyard and bears left downhill to pass a stone dovecote. Cross the River Glyme then turn left, crossing a field and going through a gate to join a track which passes Park Farm to reach the road at Over Kiddington. Turn right to the crossroads.

Walk 22: Woodstock

Start/finish: High Street, Woodstock; grid reference 445167.

Summary: An easy circular walk which gives a glimpse of Blenheim Park, includes a section of Roman road and explores a lovely old green lane whose future, in its present form, is threatened – so do this walk soon to enjoy it at its best.

Length: 5 miles/8km.

Maps: OS Landranger 164, OS Explorer 180.

Buses/coaches: Stagecoach Oxford X50 Oxford to Stratford via Woodstock, daily; 20/20A/20B/20C Oxford to Woodstock, daily (also to/from Chipping Norton, daily except Sunday); 42 Witney to Woodstock, Monday to Saturday; Worth's Motor Services 70 Oxford to Enstone via Woodstock, Monday to Saturday; the Shakespearean, a direct coach from London (Grosvenor Gardens) also operates, leaving at 9.00am and then running as the 10.50am X50 from Oxford.

Trains: Nearest station is Hanborough (bus 42 provides a link).

Parking: Public car park in Woodstock.

The Tea Shop

Harriet's Cake Shop, Patisserie and Tea Rooms, Ye Anciente House, High Street, Woodstock.

A lovely, gabled stone building, Ye Anciente House was built in 1627. Inside it's a mixture of stone, panelling and plaster, with a beamed ceiling and wooden floor. A superb array of bread and cakes is available from the shop counter, as well as gift items, biscuits and conserves. The tea room menu includes home-made soup of the day, sandwiches, ploughman's, English breakfast (served until noon) and a variety of hot snacks such as pasties, pizzas and quiches, served with salad garnish and crusty bread. Cotswold cream teas are served all day, along with scones, croissants, crumpets, home-made cakes, desserts and ice cream. There is a range of speciality teas and coffees, and the choice of cold drinks includes Blenheim mineral water. Vegetarians are catered for and the waitresses can advise on the precise ingredients. At the rear of the tea rooms is a south-facing garden, where both dogs and smokers are welcome. Open: 8.30am-5.30pm Monday to Friday; 8.30am-6.00pm Saturday; 9.30am-6.pm Sunday. Telephone: 01993 811231

Woodstock

Tourists come from all over the world to visit Blenheim Palace, probably the largest private house in Britain. Impressive it may be, but this overblown monument to military achievement could hardly be called beautiful and for many people the charming vernacular houses which grace the streets of neighbouring Woodstock are far more attractive than the impossibly grandiose palace. The grey stone buildings, their steeply pitched and gabled roofs stained green with lichen, create a harmony which makes a walk around the ancient streets a considerable pleasure.

Long before Blenheim Palace was built there was another palace at Woodstock, where the Black Prince, son of Edward III, was born c1340. From the Saxon kings to the Tudors, Woodstock was a favourite with Royalty, who used it as a base when hunting in Wychwood Forest. Sadly, there is no trace today of that early palace.

Blenheim Park

The Walk

Go down the High Street and continue along Park Street, passing the Bear Hotel, the Oxfordshire Museum and the church, before turning right on Chaucer's Lane. At a junction with Harrison's Lane go forward down steps (Hoggrove Hill) to the main road and turn left. Go along The Causeway and soon left on a bridleway, passing through dark-green wooden gates, past the back of a house then through another green gate into Blenheim Park.

Blenheim Palace was built for John Churchill, commander of the British army and first Duke of Marlborough, as a reward for a string of victories, including Blenheim in 1704, against the French. The palace was designed by Vanbrugh and sits in an immense park landscaped by Capability Brown. Marlborough's descendants still live at Blenheim. The most famous of them, Sir Winston Churchill, was born there in 1874 and now lies in the churchyard at nearby Bladon.

Turn right past Queen's Pool on a surfaced path. The palace is visible beyond the lake, which is covered in swans, geese and ducks,

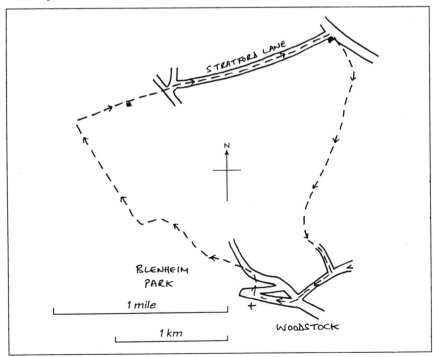

while moorhens graze the lawns beneath majestic oaks and beeches. The path quite soon bends to the left and a monument, the Column of Victory, comes into view. The path then turns sharp right and runs dead straight towards the northern edge of the park. As you approach a gate at a footpath junction, notice slight earthworks to either side of the path - this is Grim's Ditch, one of three separate earthworks of that name in Oxfordshire.

Turn right along the course of the Roman road Akeman Street, now part of the Oxfordshire Way. Go to the left of a farm, through a young plantation and across a field then turn right, and almost at once left, to leave the park through a gate in the wall. Cross the A44 with care and join a lane opposite, signed to Wootton, then almost at once turn right on another lane, signed to Bletchingdon but called Stratford Lane. Before long, green and white posts indicate a roadside verge nature reserve, and you can expect to see a good range of wild flowers in spring and summer.

The lane descends to cross the River Glyme (where the Roman "street" forded the river – hence Stratford Lane) then climbs out of the valley. At a road junction turn right by Samson's Farm (now occupied by the Oxford School of Drama) leaving both Akeman Street and the Oxfordshire Way and soon joining a bridleway on the right, which becomes a tree-lined green lane. At the time of writing the future of this delightful track is uncertain. The civil engineering charity Sustrans intends to transform it into a cycle path, and has the support of the local council, but not necessarily the local community. While cycle paths are obviously desirable they should not be created at the expense of such lovely old highways as this. Local people are fighting the plan but are not confident of success.

At a fork go right and eventually join a surfaced track. Keep on in the same direction. At a junction turn right, soon left on Union Street and then right to the town centre.

Walk 23: Eynsham

Start/finish: The Square, Eynsham; grid reference 434093.

Summary: A level circular walk in low-lying farmland near the River Thames. A highlight of the walk is the fascinating village of Stanton Harcourt and there is also an attractive stretch of the Thames Path.

Length: 8½ miles/13.7km.

Maps: OS Landranger 164, OS Explorer 180.

Buses/coaches: Stagecoach Oxford 100 Oxford to Carterton via Eynsham, daily (every 10 minutes on weekdays, half-hourly on Sundays); 11 Oxford to Witney via Eynsham, Monday to Saturday; X3 Oxford to Fulbrook via Eynsham, Monday to Saturday.

Trains: Nearest station is Hanborough.

Parking: Some spaces may be available in Eynsham village centre but please be considerate; far better to get one of the very frequent buses from Oxford.

The Tea Shop

The Granary, 11 High Street, Eynsham.

The Granary occupies a prominent position in the centre of the village and offers a warm and friendly welcome. It doubles as a baker's shop so you can choose from a wide range of cakes, scones, tea cakes, sausage rolls and all the other goods you would expect to find in a bakery. In addition, there are sandwiches, baguettes, pasties and pizza, while drinks include tea, coffee, chocolate and soft drinks. Vegetarians should find something suitable but are advised to ask for details. There is no smoking and dogs are not allowed.

Open: 8.00am-4.00pm Monday to Saturday. Telephone: 01865 884132.

Eynsham

Eynsham has grown fast in recent years but the old town is much as it ever was, with long rows of stone houses strung out along the Oxford road. It is an ancient place, with evidence of prehistoric and Roman settlement nearby, and is mentioned in the Anglo-Saxon Chronicle (as Egonesham) because it was captured by Cutwulf of Wessex in 571. In 1005 a Benedictine abbey was founded on a site near the present church. Though the abbey attained considerable importance only scattered remnants of its stonework now remain in gardens and built into walls. St Leonard's Church is an imposing building which overlooks the village square, where stands the shaft of a 13th-century market cross.

The Walk

Walk along Church Street then on along Swan Street, at the end of which turn left beside the B4449. Before you reach a junction join a footpath on the right, signed to Chilbridge Lane. This takes you past

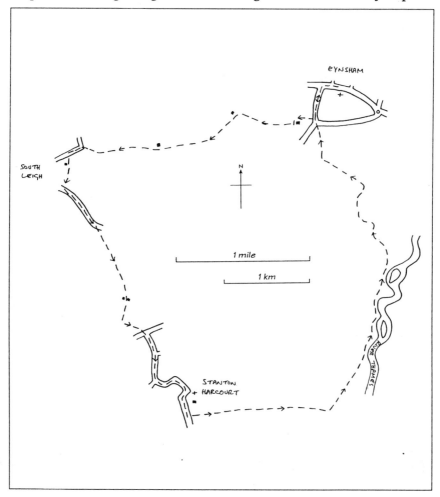

two sides of an industrial building then through a car park and along a grassy path created on the course of a dismantled railway. Just before an earthwork partially blocks the path look for a footpath on the right. This joins a track which leads towards a house where you turn left on a bridleway.

After eventually passing another house the bridleway changes from a hard-surfaced one to a grassy one but follows an obvious course across fields. At one point you briefly rejoin the old railway before joining a lane, along which you continue in the same direction, before turning left over a footbridge to join another bridleway.

Go forward along the edge of a field, past a farm and along the farm drive to a lane. Turn left, and join the second footpath on the right, just after a private road. Go diagonally across a field to a point about halfway along the far side. Go through a gap in the hedge and on through a young plantation then across arable fields towards a farm. Pass through the farmyard and straight on along the farm lane which soon makes a sharp left turn to reach a road. Go down the lane opposite towards Stanton Harcourt.

Keep straight on past a pub and at the next junction bear left to continue through the heart of the village. You'll soon come to the 12th-century church of St Michael, which is one of the most inter-

Stanton Harcourt Manor

esting in the county. It houses the shrine of St Edburg which was brought here from Bicester Priory at the Dissolution. Edburg was the daughter of King Penda of Mercia and became Abbess of Aylesbury. She died c650 but the shrine, made of Purbeck marble, dates from c1320. The church also contains a 13th-century wooden screen, a very rare survival, and possibly the oldest of its kind in England. It bears a 15th-century painting of a woman in nun's habit wearing a crown. Close by is a monument to Robert Harcourt, standard bearer to Henry Tudor at the Battle of Bosworth in 1485. His tattered flag still hangs over his tomb. There are other impressive memorials to the Harcourts, whose superb home, Stanton Harcourt Manor, is next to the church.

It was in the 12th century that Isabel de Canville, a descendant of Henry I's Queen Adela, brought the Manor of Stanton into the Harcourt family when she married Robert de Harcourt, and the house is still occupied by their descendants. A fortified manor house was built between 1380 and 1470 but has mostly disappeared. However, the Great Kitchen remains, with its unique conical roof, and so does a tower above a chapel. The kitchen is the only one of its kind in this country. It has no chimney – smoke collected in the cove of the roof and exited through wooden vents which were opened as required. There was originally a well in the centre of the kitchen but this has been filled in. The tower above the chapel, built c1460-70, is known as Pope's Tower because Alexander Pope stayed there 1717-18 while translating Homer's *Iliad*.

The house contains a notable collection of paintings, furniture, silver and porcelain, and is set in extensive gardens with formal areas, woodland, fish ponds and the remains of a moat. The house and gardens are open from April to September on certain Thursdays and Sundays and also on bank holidays. Walk past the manor then turn left on Steadys Lane which soon becomes a bridleway and runs dead straight towards the Thames. At a junction go forward on the Thames Path. Enter a field and turn left along its edge then diagonally across the next two fields to the river. Follow it north and when you come to a weir and lock leave the Thames Path, turning left towards Eynsham. The well-trodden path stays by the river for a while before bearing away from it. After making a left turn over a footbridge walk to the far right corner of a meadow, after which the route is again obvious, going forward along a green lane until a left turn leads to a surfaced bridleway. Turn right to Eynsham.

Walk 24: Minster Lovell to Witney

Start:	The White Hart, Minster Lovell; grid reference 315110.
Finish:	The Butter Cross, Witney; grid reference 356096.
Summary:	A short and very easy linear walk which introduces you to Witney and explores the romantic ruins of Minster Lovell Hall in the lush valley of the River Windrush.
Length:	3½ miles/5.6km.
Maps:	OS Landranger 164, OS Explorer 180.
Buses/coaches:	Swanbrook Coaches 53 Tewkesbury/Gloucester to Oxford via Minster Lovell and Witney, daily; Stagecoach Oxford X3 Oxford to Fulbrook via Minster Lovell and Witney, Monday to Saturday (also includes early morning journey from Milton and Shipton under Wychwood); 102/103 Witney to Carterton via Minster Lovell, Monday to Saturday; Stagecoach Oxford 100 Oxford to Carterton via Witney, daily.
Trains:	Nearest stations are Hanborough, Combe and Finstock.
Parking:	Public car parks in Witney. There is a small car park in Minster Lovell though it is really intended for visitors to the hall.

The Tea Shop

The Old Studio Coffee House, 38 High Street, Witney.

This is a welcoming, traditional place with a stone-flagged floor and beamed ceiling. There is a huge choice of meals – 14 different breakfasts, for instance, which are served all day. Other dishes include jacket potatoes, chip butties, sandwiches, pasta, fish and chips, chilli con carne, omelettes, salads and a range of daily specials. There are children's menus, cakes and pastries, ice creams, sundaes and other desserts, and a number of set morning and afternoon teas. Drinks include a good choice of coffees and specialist teas, and plenty of fruit juices, milk shakes and soft drinks. Vegetarians will be able to find something suitable from the impressive selection on offer. There are separate areas for smokers and non-smokers and guide dogs are welcome.

Open: 8.00am-5.00pm Monday to Wednesday; 8.00am-6.00pm Thursday to Saturday. Telephone: 01993 700803.

Minster Lovell

Minster Lovell is in two parts, old and new. The old village by the Windrush consists of little more than a single street of beautiful houses, culminating in a church and the ruins of Minster Lovell Hall. A substantial manor house, it was arranged around a quadrangle, which was open to the Windrush on one side. It was built for Lord William Lovell in the 1430s, replacing an earlier house (the Lovells had owned the site since the 12th century) and extended by his son Lord Francis, who was later involved in Lambert Simnel's revolt against Henry VII in 1487. Lovell may have been killed at the subsequent Battle of Stoke, but legend claims that he escaped and hid in a secret room in the hall, only to be trapped when his faithful servant unexpectedly died. In 1708 workmen found a man's skeleton seated at a desk in an underground room. The hall was abandoned after the last resident, Thomas Coke, Earl of Leicester, moved to Norfolk in the 1740s.

Minster Lovell Hall and Church

The Walk

Take the bus to Minster Lovell and get off at the White Hart. Walk down a footpath to the right of School Lane and turn right when you reach a road. Cross the Windrush and then decide whether you wish to walk along the village street or across fields. For the village street walk up to the Swan Inn and turn right. If you prefer to walk across the fields join a footpath just to the north of the river. It takes you across Wash Meadow to the far left corner. Keep forward along field edges until you reach the church and the ruins of Minster Lovell Hall.

When you're ready to proceed, a kissing gate at the far corner of the site gives access to a footpath (another path here allows you to visit a 15th-century dovecote at Manor Farm if you wish). The path leads quickly to a stile and footbridge then follows a well-defined course across a field until another footbridge crosses the Windrush. Climb up a bank and follow the path to a junction where you continue forward beside the river, soon turning right to cross a tributary

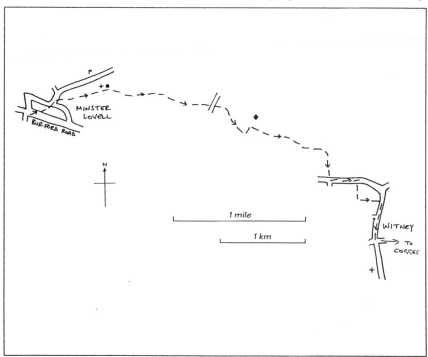

and then turning left through a plantation and into a meadow. Go forward by the right-hand hedge on a waymarked route with frequent stiles. Eventually you bear right uphill through light woodland (Maggots Grove). At the top of the wood go through a field to a lane and cross to find a footpath and bridleway. Take the latter, which descends towards the Windrush. Reaching the valley, turn right and walk between a fence and a line of willows, soon forking left on a footpath which runs alongside a stream. At the far side of the field turn left towards a large mill then turn right alongside the Windrush.

Follow the river to a point where a pipe crosses it. Bear right here, crossing a stream and then turning left on a path. After passing through a gate go along a green lane to a junction where you go second right, climbing gently on a sandy track. At the main road, turn left past Early's factory and mill, established in 1670. Turn right on Puck Lane and left at a junction to reach High Street. Turn right to find the Old Studio Coffee House.

Witney

The chief town of West Oxfordshire, Witney has been famous for blanket making since the Middle Ages. The oldest blanket works in town today is Early Mill, which has been in production for over 300 years. Witney's main street is over a mile long, flanked by stone buildings of considerable charm. A focal point is provided by the 17th-century Butter Cross in Market Square. To the south of this a wide green flanked by elegant houses leads to the majestic church. The excavated remains of a 12th-century palace of the Bishop of Winchester lie nearby within the grounds of Mount House. It's open to the public from Easter to mid September, Saturday and Sunday afternoons only.

A worthwhile extension to the walk can be made by going down Langdale Gate (near the Butter Cross) to visit St Mary's Church and Manor Farm Museum (open April to October), a working Victorian farm museum in a partly medieval farmhouse just across the Windrush at the hamlet of Cogges.

Walk 25: Minster Lovell to Burford

Start: The White Hart, Minster Lovell; grid reference 315110.

Finish: High Street, Burford; grid reference 252123.

Summary: A linear walk of exceptional interest, passing through picturesque and fascinating villages in the valley of the Windrush before finishing in Burford, one of the loveliest of Cotswold towns.

Length: 7 miles/11.2km.

Maps: OS Landrangers 163 and 164; OS Outdoor Leisure 45 and OS Explorer 180 (each shows part of route).

Buses/coaches: Swanbrook Coaches 53 Tewkesbury/Gloucester to Oxford via Minster Lovell and Burford, daily; Stagecoach Oxford X3 Oxford to Fulbrook via Minster Lovell and Burford, Monday to Saturday (also includes early morning journey from Milton and Shipton under Wychwood); 102/103 Witney to Carterton via Minster Lovell, Monday to Saturday.

Trains: Nearest station is Shipton under Wychwood (though few trains stop there; Charlbury isn't much further but Oxford is best for bus connections).

Parking: Public car park in Burford, and there's also a car park near Minster Lovell Hall but it is really meant for visitors to the hall.

The Tea Shop

Huffkins, 98 High Street, Burford.

Housed in a lovely stone building with red and white paintwork, Huffkins functions as a bakery and patisserie as well as a tea room. The interior walls are stone below a beamed ceiling, and decoration is provided by Victorian prints, antique china, pewterware and teapots. Warm and welcoming, it is always busy, but there is plenty of seating. The menu is wide-ranging, with snacks such as soup, jacket potatoes and sandwiches always available. Very sensibly, "afternoon teas" are served all day – choose from a set menu or just have a cake, scone or pastry from the delicious selection on offer. Everything is freshly made in Huffkins' bakery. Lunches and breakfasts are also served all day, and the breakfast choices include traditional and "Cotswold" (kippers!), amongst others. There is so much choice

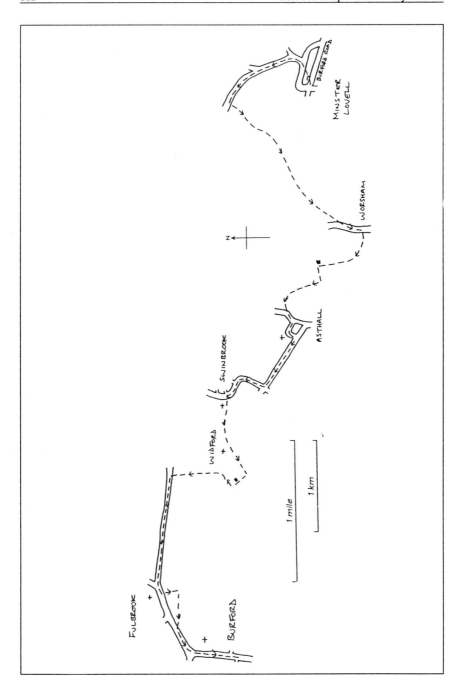

that vegetarians are certain to find something and Mr and Mrs Plank claim to "cater for everyone". There is a good selection of drinks and tea comes in generous pots with extra hot water. Smoking is not permitted. Guide dogs are welcome in the shop, and other dogs may be welcome in the garden which is open only in summer.

Open: 9.00am-5.30pm Monday to Friday; 9.00am-6.00pm Saturday. Telephone: 01993 822126.

Minster Lovell

For information about Minster Lovell please see Walk 24.

The Walk

Get off the bus at the White Hart at Minster Lovell and go down a footpath to the right of School Lane. Turn right, cross the Windrush and walk up the lane, passing the Swan Inn and Minster Lovell Mill. The lane climbs gently to a junction where you turn left on a high-banked lane. When you reach a bridleway turn left onto it. Reed-fringed in places, it follows the Windrush upstream for about a mile (1.6km) to join a lane near Worsham Mill.

Turn left, crossing the river, then shortly right on another bridleway, which is easily followed to Asthall Farm. The lovely old farmhouse is built on the Roman road Akeman Street. Turn left to reach a lane, left again then right by the tiny village green at Asthall to St Nicholas' Church, which is of great architectural interest and beauty, with work from every major church-building period from Norman onwards. The "bird beak" carvings inside are superb and very rare. The stone altar has a built-in piscina, also said to be very rare, if not unique. There is a remarkable clock made by a blacksmith c1665-80. The churchyard contains a multitude of excellent 17th- and 18th-century tombstones. The manor house close by the church was built in 1620.

Leaving the churchyard, turn right up the lane, and soon right again. Walk to a crossroads and turn right once more, crossing the Windrush to enter Swinbrook. The Swan Inn dates from the 16th century, there is a magnificent barn at Old Farm and St Mary's Church is a real gem. Outside, there are tea caddy tombs and entertaining headstones carved with cherubs and skulls. Just west of the church porch is the grave of author Nancy Mitford (1904-73), her headstone inscribed with the family symbol, a mole. Next to her lies

The Fettiplace Memorial

her sister, Unity Valkyrie Mitford (1914-48), notorious for her associations with Nazi Germany. Inside the church are two captivating and very famous trios of reclining figures, the Fettiplace effigies, strangely stacked in tiers and sculptured in 1613 and 1686. Note how very different in style they are, with the later trio appearing far more natural.

Exit the churchyard by a small white gate where a sign points the way to St Oswald's at Widford. Beside the footpath are traces of the fishponds and terraces which are all that remain of Swinbrook Manor, once the finest Tudor house in Oxfordshire but long since destroyed. A well-trodden route leads across sheep pasture to the church at Widford, all around which are earthworks revealing the site of a deserted medieval village. The church was built by the monks of St Oswald's Priory, Gloucester (Widford belonged to Gloucestershire until 1844) on the site of a Roman villa. When the church was restored in 1904 a tessellated Roman pavement was discovered, but has been covered up for its own protection. Medieval wall paintings were also discovered, some dating from 1350.

Rejoin the footpath to reach a lane and turn right, passing a lovely 17th-century house then joining a bridleway. This soon bends to the right and takes you round a field edge to a lane. Turn left, enjoying good views across the Windrush valley until the lane descends into Fulbrook, another charming village. The church is Norman with traces of Saxon work, and outside it there stands a huge yew tree about 1000 years old.

Turn left on Meadow Lane, shortly bearing right onto a footpath which leads back to the road. Turn left for Burford, where you'll find Huffkins halfway up High Street on the right-hand side.

Burford

The town's origins lie in the Saxon period, when a ford on the Windrush was part of an important route linking Wessex and Mercia, but it was the wool trade which made Burford rich. Many of the houses along the beautiful High Street were built by medieval wool merchants, though some acquired new façades in the Georgian era. With its golden stone frontages, wonderfully irregular roof-line, and the manner in which it plunges headlong downhill, only to end abruptly by the Windrush, High Street is unforgettable, but there are also numerous side streets, alleys and courts to explore. Sheep Street, for instance, should not be missed.

The church, built between 1160 and 1475, contains an incredible range of monuments, brasses, carvings and other details of great interest. It deserves a book to itself, but fortunately an excellent range of leaflets and booklets is available in the church, with information on all its many features. Like nearly all our medieval churches, that at Burford suffered from Victorian "restoration", and it was the work carried out here by the architect Street that was the catalyst which caused William Morris to establish the Society for the Protection of Ancient Buildings.

Walk 26: Filkins

Start/finish:	Cotswold Woollen Weavers, Filkins; grid reference 240045.
Summary:	Level and easy, much of this circular walk on the Cotswold fringe is on quiet lanes, the rest on well-defined footpaths. Though very short, it could take some time to complete because it visits four delightful villages where there is lots to see.
Length:	3½ miles/5.6km.
Maps:	OS Landranger 163, OS Outdoor Leisure 45.
Buses/coaches:	Stagecoach Oxford 64 Carterton to Swindon via Filkins, Monday to Saturday; 7 Witney to Swindon via Filkins, Sunday; Stagecoach buses run from Oxford to Carterton and Witney every few minutes, providing frequent connections.
Trains:	Nearest station is Swindon.
Parking:	Cotswold Woollen Weavers.

The Tea Shop

Cotswold Woollen Weavers, Filkins.

Cotswold wealth was based on the wool trade for centuries. There may be fewer sheep around these days but at Filkins the tradition of fine woollens continues. Cotswold Woollen Weavers make a wide range of woollen garments and soft furnishings on traditional machinery in an 18th-century barn. You can watch the manufacturing process in action (there is no admittance charge) then buy the finished products in the well-stocked mill shop. There are also exhibitions, a picnic area and, of course, the coffee shop. It's only small, but attractively fitted out in a converted barn. The menu includes home-made soup and ploughman's lunches or you can choose from an appetising range of cakes and scones. Drinks include coffee, tea, herbal teas, fruit juice, squash, milk and mineral water. No specific effort is made to cater for vegetarians but some of the products will be suitable so ask for details. There are smoking and no smoking areas. The only dogs permitted are guide dogs.

Open: 10.00am-6.00pm Monday to Saturday; 2.00pm-6.00pm Sunday. Closed Christmas week. Telephone: 01367 860491.

Filkins and Broughton Poggs

The two villages lie adjacent to each other, divided only by the Broadwell Brook, on which stands Broughton Poggs Mill. The appealingly named Broughton Poggs is much the smaller village, but has the better church – a simple building with what is probably a pre-Conquest saddleback tower. Filkins is full of delightful houses, ranging from the humble to the grand, but all in the same harmonious stone. Many of the gardens are attractively fenced with upright slabs of stone. The fascinating Swinford Museum was set up in the 1920s to display local domestic, agricultural, trade and craft tools in a 17th-century cottage. Opening times are limited: call 01367 860334 for details.

St Peter's Church, Broughton Poggs

The Walk

With your back to Cotswold Woollen Weavers turn right through the village. At a junction near a pub keep straight on, passing to the left of the church and shortly forking left to pass between two houses whose owners seem to be engaged in a topiary competition.

At a junction go forward to pass Broughton Poggs Mill and cross to the driveway to Broughton Hall. It soon bends to the left and you come to a grassy triangle. Fork left to find a gate hidden behind yew trees and go through to find a path to St Peter's Church, classic in its simplicity and standing adjacent to a farmyard.

Retrace your steps to Broughton Poggs Mill and turn right. Soon after passing a house called Filkins Moor join a footpath on the right which runs through a tiny Woodland Trust nature reserve, dedicated to the memory of Leonard George Samsworth of Oxford (1920-91). A gate opens into a field where you go obliquely left towards a stile near the left-hand end of a row of poplars. Turn right, either along a lane, or along a footpath which runs parallel with it just the other side of the opposite hedge. The footpath rejoins the lane after passing through a strip of woodland.

Soon after passing Filkins Mill join a footpath on the left. Follow the left-hand field edge as far as a cross-field hedge, go through a gap and then towards the far right corner of the next field and over a stile. Go forward to a lane. Turn right into Langford, noting a footpath on

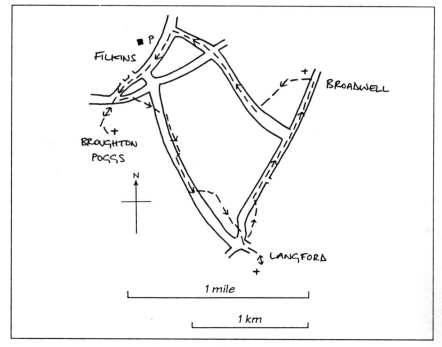

the left after a few paces; this is the return route to Filkins, but Langford is worth the short detour first. In St Matthew's Church it possesses one of England's finest Saxon churches, with many rare and remarkable features. Having explored the village, return to the footpath mentioned above. It bears left over two fields to return you to the lane. Turn right into Broadwell.

This is yet another attractive village, also with an interesting church. The tower and spire date from 1250 and there is a finely carved Norman doorway. Walk through the churchyard and leave through a small gate. Pass to the left of a pond and, when you reach a track, turn right, then shortly bear left towards a stile. Climb over then turn left across a long, narrow field, close to its right-hand edge.

A stile gives onto a lane, where you turn right. Cross the main road with care and walk along the lane opposite, soon following it round to the left, and passing some very impressive houses as you return to Filkins.

Walk 27: Lechlade

Start/finish: Market Place, Lechlade; grid reference 215995.

Summary: This delightful circular walk includes a particularly lovely stretch of the River Thames. Though the walk starts and finishes in Gloucestershire, and takes in a tiny bit of Wiltshire, the middle section includes two charming Oxfordshire villages, one of which was home to the great William Morris.

Length: 9 miles/14.5km.

Maps: OS Landranger 163, OS Explorer 170.

Buses/coaches: Stagecoach Oxford 64 Witney/Carterton to Swindon via Lechlade, Monday to Saturday; 7 Witney to Swindon via Lechlade, Sundays; Stagecoach Swindon & District 77 Cirencester to Swindon via Lechlade, Monday to Saturday; Thamesdown 67 Swindon to Ashbury via Buscot, Fridays.

Trains: Nearest station is Swindon.

Parking: Public car park in Lechlade.

The Tea Shop

Village Shop and Tea Room, Buscot.

Barney the shop cat presides (when he isn't busy elsewhere) over this small tea room tucked into Brenda Bomford's well-stocked village shop. A warm welcome, flowery tablecloths and stencilled wall paintings (including a brilliant one of Barney) help create a pleasant atmosphere in which to enjoy a snack and a drink. There is also outside seating at picnic tables in a pretty garden. Choose from soup, sandwiches, sausage rolls, pies, pasties, cream teas, cakes, scones or ice cream. Drinks include tea, coffee and soft drinks. Many of the items on offer are suitable for vegetarians – Brenda uses free-range eggs, veggie cheese, butter or vegetable margarine and vegetable stock. Dogs are welcome in the garden, but there is no smoking.

Open: 10.00am-5.30pm Tuesday to Saturday; 12.00am-5.30pm Sunday; 12.00am-6.00pm bank holidays. Telephone: 01367 252142.

Lechlade

Lechlade lies at an ancient road junction on the edge of the Cotswolds but its character derives more from its situation at the confluence of four rivers – Coln, Cole, Leach and Thames. After the completion in 1789 of the Thames and Severn Canal, Lechlade became even more of a waterside town, and that's still how it seems today, though the canal is now disused and neither Coln, Cole nor Leach make a very obvious impact on visitors. The Thames is a more magnetic draw, but before you go down to the river do explore the old town, which is packed with buildings of considerable interest, some of them built with the proceeds of the wool trade, while others date from the coaching era. Though much of Lechlade's wealth derived from wool, the wharves were also busy with barges laden with stone, cheese and corn bound for London and Bristol. There are no commercial craft today, but the Thames is still busy with pleasure boats and there is a colourful marina.

St John's Lock, Lechlade

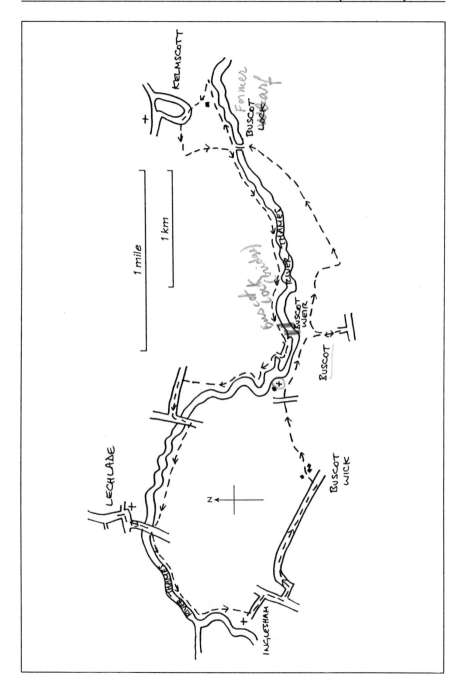

The Walk

Walk along the High Street then turn down Thames Street. Cross the river on Ha'penny Bridge (a former tollbridge) and turn right on the Thames Path, soon reaching its confluence with the River Coln. The Thames and Severn Canal was joined to the Thames here too, and an 18th-century roundhouse, built for the canal lengthman, still marks the spot.

After crossing a footbridge, the Thames Path leads to the tiny settlement of Inglesham, then to the road. Turn right, shortly leaving the Thames Path to turn left on a lane to Buscot. A little way along here you cross the River Cole and enter Oxfordshire.

Turn left on a bridleway when you come to Buscot Wick. After passing a tree surrounded by staddle stones turn right past the second of two houses. As you approach the entrance to a third, branch right to a bridle gate. Walk past the house then turn left. The path now goes obliquely right to pass through a gate and on across a big field, past a solitary tree to another gate beneath a large oak. Follow a field edge to the left to another gate and cut the corner of one final field to the road. Go into another field opposite and bear right to pass a fine Queen Anne house, Buscot Parsonage (National Trust). Cross the driveway and enter Buscot churchyard. The church has a Norman chancel arch and a window by William Morris's associate Burne-Jones.

Leave the churchyard by the lychgate and walk across a meadow, with the Thames now on your left. At Buscot Weir turn right, passing the National Trust's Buscot Weir Field (a popular picnic spot) and continuing to Buscot village, an attractive little place of grey stone and orange brick. Having visited the tea shop, retrace your steps a little way before turning right along the edge of Buscot Weir Field, over a footbridge into another field and straight on. Over on the left is a pillbox, one of many along this stretch of the Thames. Apparently, they were intended as a last line of defence in the event of a German invasion, which seems a bit optimistic. If Hitler had got this far, a string of pillboxes would hardly have stopped him.

Coming to a track at the site of the former Buscot Wharf, turn right. Just as the track joins a road turn left on a footpath running diagonally across fields. After crossing a footbridge the path bears right and continues by a left-hand field edge until eventually a signpost directs you left towards the river. Cross at Buscot Lock and turn right on the Thames Path.

After crossing a footbridge leave the Thames Path, turning left into Kelmscott, which will forever be associated with the name of William Morris (1834-96): artist, designer, craftsman, writer, poet and socialist. The beautiful 16th-century Kelmscott Manor, its gardens sweeping down to the Thames, was his summer home from 1871 until his death in 1896. Owned by the Society of Antiquaries, it is open to the public, but on a limited basis (call 01367 252486). It exhibits an impressive collection of textiles, ceramics, furniture and other items associated with Morris's Arts and Crafts Movement and the Pre-Raphaelites. Morris and his wife Jane are buried in the village churchyard. Following the lane through Kelmscott, it is easy to see why Morris was so taken by this dream village.

Turn right past the Plough Inn to join a footpath signed to Buscot Lock. Once back at the lock, rejoin the Thames Path, turning right. The path closely follows the meandering river until eventually leading away from it to a road. Turn left, then soon left again over St John's Bridge to rejoin the towpath for the short stroll into Lechlade.

sentier
de Halage

Walk 28: Faringdon

Start/finish:	Market Place, Faringdon; grid reference 289956.
Summary:	An undemanding circular walk in pleasant countryside with some fine views. There is much of historical and architectural interest, including one of the finest monastic barns in the country.
Length:	7 miles/11.2km.
Maps:	OS Landrangers 163 and 174, OS Explorer 170.
Buses/coaches:	Stagecoach Swindon & District 66 Swindon to Oxford via Faringdon, Monday to Saturday; Stagecoach Oxford 63/65/65A/X65 Oxford/ Wantage/Abingdon to Swindon via Faringdon, Monday to Saturday.
Trains:	Nearest station is Swindon.
Parking:	Public car parks in Faringdon.

The Tea Shop

Faringdon Wholefoods and Coffee Shop, 4B Market Place, Faringdon.

The tea room occupies a lovely building in an elevated position above the Market Place. Bright and friendly, with fresh flowers on the tables and dried flowers suspended from the ceiling beams, this is a pleasant place which has already become popular with walkers. Choose from an appetising selection of light meals, including home-made soup, sandwiches, toasted sandwiches, quiches, cakes, scones etc. A good range of hot and cold drinks includes elderflower pressé and some delicious fruit juices. There are always vegetarian choices available, such as quiches and pasties. All soups are made with vegetable stock and only free-range eggs are used. Everything is reasonably priced and the shop has an extensive range of herbal teas, spices, nuts, seeds, dried fruits and local specialities such as cheese and honey. Guide dogs are welcome and other dogs "within reason" but there is strictly no smoking.

Open: 9.30am-5.00pm daily. Telephone: 01367 241574.

Faringdon

This unspoiled market town sits on the limestone ridge which extends towards Oxford from Wiltshire and consequently it has the benefit of some fine views. Alfred the Great may have thought so too as he had a palace here, but it was King John who granted Faringdon its market charter in 1218. The town became important because of its position on the London to Cirencester road and it prospered during the 15th and 16th centuries but was badly damaged during the Civil War. Much of the present town dates from the 17th and 18th centuries, and forms a charming cluster of elegant houses round the old market place, where the 17th-century town hall provides a focal point. The 13th-century church sits on a slight rise nearby and next to it is impressive Faringdon House, built for Henry Pye, Poet Laureate to George III.

The Walk

Leave the Market Place on London Street and turn right on Stanford Road. Take the first footpath on the left, which leads to Folly Hill, crowned with a tower. This is Faringdon Folly, built in 1935 by Lord Berners as a birthday gift for Robert Heber-Percy (who later inherited Faringdon House). It provided work for local men unemployed during the Great Depression, but not everybody approved – "Lord Berners' monstrous erection" was one local view.

Carry on past the tower towards the bypass until you come to a footpath junction. Turn right along a well-trodden path which leads eventually to the bypass. Cross with care, turn right and then left on a footway by the A417.

Shortly turn right on a bridleway to Little Coxwell, following a clear track which leads downfield, across a brook and straight on for a little way before turning right to cross a former railway bridge. Continue past a farm and keep straight on at a bridleway junction to reach Fernham Road. Turn left, then right into Little Coxwell.

Follow the lane through the village (look for the warthog on the roof of Capers Cottage) and then follow it to the right to reach the A420. Turn right and cross with great care to a footpath next to a house. The path runs directly towards Great Coxwell, but as you reach the edge of the village turn left to enter the churchyard. 12th-century St Giles' Church has a superb 14th-century door with Perpendicular tracery on it and inside are some charming memorial brasses.

Leaving the churchyard turn right through the village, soon reaching the famous Great Barn and the beautiful Court House next to it.

The barn, now owned by the National Trust, is a 13th-century Cistercian monastic building and its interior roof construction is probably unequalled in this country. William Morris, who lived nearby at Kelmscott, called it "the finest piece of architecture in England". Coxwell was a monastic grange of Beaulieu Abbey and this barn must originally have been just one of several similarly magnificent buildings on the site.

A footpath passes the end of the barn and continues past a pond to enter a field. Turn right along the field edge before cutting through woodland to another field. Turn right to reach a road. Cross to a permissive footpath opposite which leads along a field edge to Badbury Wood, just to the left. Walk to an information panel and join a footpath signed next to it.

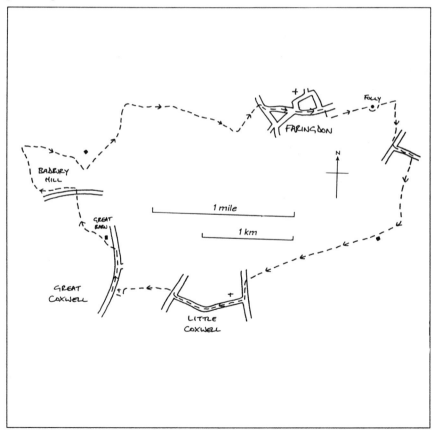

Badbury Wood is owned by the National Trust and managed by the Forestry Commission for commercial, wildlife and leisure use. The wood clothes Badbury Hill which is capped with beech trees growing on the ramparts of an Iron Age settlement about 2500 years old. Buzzards are likely to be seen overhead, while roe and fallow deer inhabit the wood.

The footpath leads past a cottage and a number of branching paths. Stay on the main path, which soon begins to descend. When you come to a stile in a new fence on the right cross it to join another footpath which leads across a felled area to another stile, after which it runs along woodland edge to meet a lane. Turn right and soon left, on a bridleway signed to Step Farm. Go straight ahead over pasture, passing to the right of Badbury Hill House.

When you come to a stile and a junction with a footpath bear left across a field to pass a wood and reach the far corner then turn right to follow a hedge to a pair of stiles and a footbridge taking you into another field. Follow power lines across here then over a stile and on along the right-hand edge of the next field. In the corner, turn left to find a stile giving onto a green lane. Follow this to the edge of Faringdon, turn left and at a T-junction turn right, then soon left into the centre.

Young rabbit, Faringdon

Walk 29: Wantage

Start/finish: Market Place, Wantage; grid reference 398879.

Summary: A longer and more strenuous walk than most in this book, though still not particularly demanding, just rather exposed in bad weather. It involves a steady climb up onto the Ridgeway, an invigorating walk along this most ancient of tracks and then a descent through two delightful villages.

Length: 8½ miles/13.7km.

Maps: OS Landranger 174, OS Explorer 170.

Buses/coaches: Stagecoach Oxford 31/31A/31B/31C/X31 Oxford/Abingdon to Wantage, daily; 32/32A/32B/X35 Oxford/Didcot to Wantage, daily; 36/37 Didcot to Wantage, Monday to Saturday; also a variety of less frequent services from Faringdon, Swindon, Stanford in the Vale; the Ridgeway Explorer from Swindon (Stagecoach Swindon & District X47) and from Reading (Weavaway Travel X48), Sundays/BHMs April to October.

Trains: Nearest station is Didcot.

Parking: Public car parks in Wantage.

The Tea Shop

The Flying Teapot, 29-30 Market Place, Wantage.

Welcoming, great value and popular with both locals and walkers, this is an unassuming and unpretentious little café, tucked away in a quiet corner between the Market Place and the church. Cheerful yellow-painted walls provide the backdrop for a collection of bizarre teapots arranged on an oak dresser and friendly young staff serve a comprehensive range of dishes. Snack meals, mostly served with chips, include eggs or beans on toast, doorstep sandwiches, salads, pies, soup, jacket potatoes, bacon butties and veggie-burgers. Also available are full English breakfasts, desserts, tempting home-made cakes, children's meals and pensioners' specials. Neither free range eggs nor veggie cheese are used, but vegetarians should find something suitable (ask for details). Hot and cold drinks are on offer at reasonable prices and if you ask for a milky coffee you get a great mugful overflowing with foaming froth – far superior to any over-priced cappuccino in a trendy coffee bar. There are smoking and no-smoking areas, but dogs are not permitted.

Open: 9.00am-5.30pm Monday to Saturday. Telephone: 01235 764164.

Wantage

Roman remains have been found at Wantage, which lies on the Portway, an ancient road running below the downs. But it was in the Saxon period that the town developed, and it is famous as the birth-place in 849 of Alfred the Great, whose statue dominates the Market

Place. Wantage was sacked by the Danes in 1001 but prospered through the Middle Ages, though most of the charming buildings which surround Alfred are of the 17th and 18th centuries. The 13th-century church was restored by the Victorian architect Street who lived in Wantage for a time. It contains tombs of the Fitzwaryn family, into which Dick Whittington married. Near the church a former cloth merchant's house is occupied by the award-winning Vale and Downland Museum, well worth a visit if you would like to know more about the area.

Alfred the Great, Wantage

The Walk

Leave Wantage on Wallingford Street and keep on past St Andrew's School. Turn right by the BP garage, and go straight on at the junction with Ormond Road, joining Charlton Road. When you come to a mini-roundabout turn right on Lark Hill, a "no through road" which climbs steadily until, having passed a farm, it levels out before descending and then climbing once more, providing extensive downland views.

When you reach a road cross to join a bridleway on the right. Shortly after passing Fursewick Farm a path crosses the bridleway. Turn left across a field, climbing again. Pass through a line of trees and on in the same direction, to the left of more trees and a fence and then straight on to join a wide bridleway at a junction. Go forward up

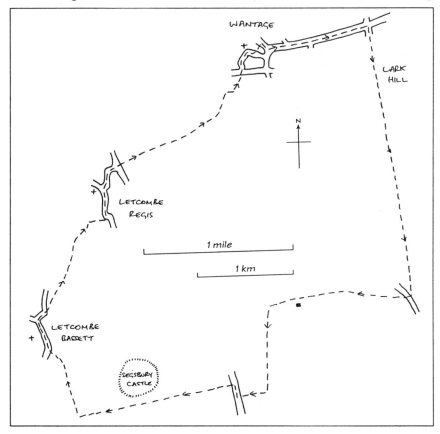

the "private road" (a public footpath) opposite, which takes you to the Ridgeway. Turn right.

At the road turn right then cross to pick up the Ridgeway again. It soon passes Segsbury Castle, an Iron Age fort commanding fine views of the Vale of White Horse. Turn right on a footpath when you come to a stile and a notice about a Countryside Stewardship site. A map here shows the extent of the access area but to continue the walk go downhill on a clear path, keeping roughly straight on. Just after a brief rise a path branches right into trees but ignore this and keep forward to join a lane where you turn right and descend to Letcombe Bassett, a village with some exquisite houses. It was immortalised as Cresscombe in Thomas Hardy's *Jude the Obscure*. Together with neighbouring Letcombe Regis it was once famous for its watercress and the spring-fed cress beds may still be seen along Letcombe Brook.

At a junction turn right towards Letcombe Regis but when you reach Rectory Lane go forward to join a footpath, which then turns left along the top of a bank above the lane. Eventually you pass a gate into a nature reserve provided by Dow AgroScience, which has a research laboratory in Letcombe Regis. The footpath leads to a junction by another Countryside Stewardship site. Turn left, then right to reach a lane and turn left into Letcombe Regis. Turn right at a junction by the church and follow the lane through the village until you come to a junction with the Wantage road. Go straight on along Manor Fields to join a surfaced footpath which leads to Wantage, passing old cress beds and The Mead, where Sir John Betjeman lived.

Reaching a road on the edge of town cross over and go along Priory Road, which twists to the left and then right before emerging by the church, beyond which is The Flying Teapot.

Walk 30: Ardington

Start/finish: High Street, Ardington; grid reference 433884.

Summary: A superb circular walk which includes three attractive villages, racehorse country, a fine stretch of the Wessex Downs and a delightful green lane beside Ginge Brook. There are some permissive paths between Ardington and Lockinge which you may use to vary or extend the walk if you wish.

Length: 7½ miles/12km.

Maps: OS Landranger 174, OS Explorer 170.

Buses/coaches: Stagecoach Oxford 32/32A/32B/X35 Oxford/Didcot to Wantage via West Hendred, daily; 36/37 Didcot to Wantage via Ardington, Monday to Saturday; W5 from Wantage to Lockinge, Monday to Saturday.

Trains: Nearest station is Didcot.

Parking: There are several possible parking places on or close to the High Street but please be considerate.

The Tea Shop

Cobwebs Tearoom, Post Office and Stores, High Street, Ardington. Ardington is an estate village with a number of mock-Tudor buildings, of which the post office stores is one. It's the very model of what a village shop should be: well-stocked, reasonably priced and friendly. The tea room consists of two tables in a screened-off corner of the shop and you can choose what you want from the shelves (a tin of soup, for instance) and they'll heat it up for you. Also available are jacket potatoes, pies, sandwiches and an excellent choice of cakes and baked goods, and cream teas in the afternoons, as well as a range of hot and cold drinks. No special attempt is made to cater for vegetarians but some items will be suitable so do ask for details. There are picnic tables outside, where dogs are welcome and smoking is permitted.

Open: 8.30am-1.15pm and 2.00pm-5.15pm Monday, Tuesday, Wednesday and Friday; 8.30pm-1.00pm Thursday. 8.30am-1.00pm and 2.15pm-5.15pm summer Saturdays (Easter – September). 8.30pm-1.00pm winter Saturdays. 9.30am-12.00am and 2.00pm-5.15pm (all day if hot) summer Sundays. 9.30am-11am winter Sundays. Telephone: 01235 833237.

Ardington

Ardington and Lockinge

Like Wantage, Ardington stands astride the ancient Portway by the foot of the downs. The village is grouped attractively round the church, which has some splendid Norman carvings. Both Ardington and neighbouring Lockinge are estate villages restored and rebuilt by the paternalistic landowner Lord Wantage (1832-1901), who earned himself a Victoria Cross in the Crimean War. He established a model farm at Lockinge and provided estate workers with decent cottages. He was also responsible for the planting of many of the hedges, copses and shelter belts in the area and he paid for the statue of King Alfred in Wantage.

The Walk

With your back to Cobwebs turn right along the High Street, then left down Well Street. Having crossed Ardington Brook turn right on a footpath and when it forks carry straight on, keeping to the left of the complex of buildings at Ardington Mill then to the left of a large brick house. The well-trodden path eventually turns right to a lane where you turn left towards East Lockinge, then first right to West

Lockinge. Having passed the main buildings of West Lockinge Farm turn left on a bridleway which passes to the right of some handsome brick and timber stables, over the doors of which Henrietta Knight's beautiful racehorses look down their aristocratic noses at passing walkers.

The bridleway continues beside willow-fringed Goddard's Brook until, at Goddard's Barn, the brook is left behind and the bridleway continues its almost imperceptible climb up to the downs. At a junction go forward up a grassy slope to intercept the Ridgeway where

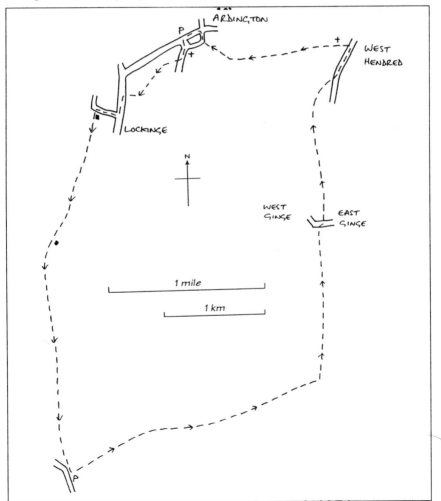

you turn left, soon passing a monument to Lord Wantage. Running alongside the Ridgeway, but lower, is Grim's Ditch, a prehistoric earthwork (one of three by this name in Oxfordshire) which runs from nearby Lattin Down to Streatley and may have acted as a stock boundary for the downsfolk.

These downs were once entirely sheepwalk but there are now large areas of gallops for the training of racehorses, and, even worse, more and more of the old flower-rich downland is being ploughed for cereal production.

Ignore a bridleway which crosses the Ridgeway just before a wood and continue to a second bridleway at East Ginge Down, its signpost visible ahead just beyond the wood. Turn left here and follow the well-defined and increasingly delightful track down to join a concrete lane at Upper Farm. Follow it to a T-junction and turn right, then left on a footpath. This lovely path runs above Ginge Brook, partly through woods of box and elder.

Eventually you come to a large arable field. Continue along its edge until you draw almost level with a terrace of houses. Turn towards them but very soon go diagonally left between vegetable plots and chicken runs to find a fenced path which takes you to a lane. Turn left into the charming village of West Hendred. At a junction by a thatched cottage turn left to the 14th-century church, joining a footpath which follows a clear route across fields then by Ardington Brook and past the impressive Ardington House to return you to the village.

Tea Shop Walks - Spreading everywhere!

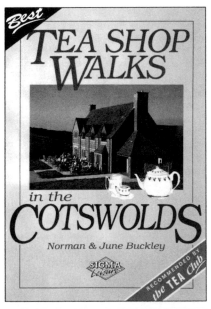

The Sigma Leisure Tea Shop Walks series already includes:

Cheshire

The Chilterns

The Cotswolds

The Lake District, Volume 1

The Lake District, Volume 2

Lancashire

Leicestershire & Rutland

North Devon

The Peak District

Shropshire

Snowdonia

South Devon

Staffordshire

Surrey & Sussex

Warwickshire

Worcestershire

The Yorkshire Dales

Each book costs £6.95 and contains an average of 25 excellent walks: far better value than any competitor!

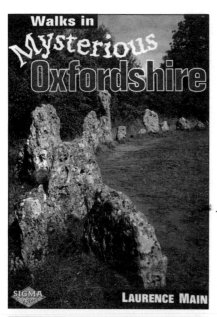

Walks in Mysterious Oxfordshire

LAURENCE MAIN

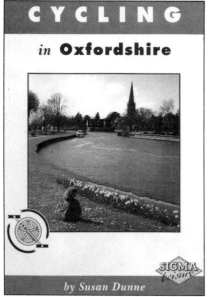

CYCLING *in* **Oxfordshire**

by Susan Dunne